FOLLOWING JESUS IN A DIGITAL AGE

Biblical Wisdom for Digital Culture

Jason Thacker

Lifeway Press® · Brentwood, Tennessee

PRODUCTION TEAM

Jason Thacker
Writer

Reid Patton
Senior Editor

Angel Prohaska
Associate Editor

Jon Rodda
Art Director

Tyler Quillet
Managing Editor

Joel Polk
Publisher, Small Group Publishing

Brian Daniel
Director, Adult Ministry Publishing

Published by Lifeway Press® • © 2022 Jason Thacker

ISBN 978-1-0877-7180-9 • Item 005839203

Dewey decimal classification: 261.5
Subject headings: TECHNOLOGY / CHRISTIAN LIFE / CULTURE

Unless indicated otherwise, Scripture quotations are taken from the Christian Standard Bible®, Copyright © 2017 by Holman Bible Publishers. Used by permission. Christian Standard Bible® and CSB® are federally registered trademarks of Holman Bible Publishers.

To order additional copies of this resource, write to Lifeway Resources Customer Service; 200 Powell Place, Suite 100; Brentwood, TN 37027; fax 615-251-5933; call toll free 800-458-2772; order online at lifeway.com; email orderentry@lifeway.com.

Printed in the United States of America

Adult Ministry Publishing • Lifeway Resources • 200 Powell Place, Suite 100 • Brentwood, TN 37027

CONTENTS

ABOUT THE AUTHOR

 **JASON THACKER** serves as chair of research in technology ethics and director of the research institute at the Ethics and Religious Liberty Commission (ERLC) of the Southern Baptist Convention. He also serves as an adjunct instructor of philosophy, ethics, and worldview at Boyce College in Louisville, Kentucky. He is the author of several books including *Following Jesus in a Digital Age* and *The Age of AI: Artificial Intelligence and the Future of Humanity*. He also serves as the editor of *The Digital Public Square: Christian Ethics in a Technological Society* releasing in 2023.

He is a graduate of the University of Tennessee in Knoxville and the Southern Baptist Theological Seminary, where he is currently pursuing a PhD in ethics, public theology, and philosophy. He serves as an associate fellow with the Kirby Laing Centre for Public Theology in Cambridge, an advisor for AI and Faith, and a research fellow with the ERLC Research Institute.

VIDEO CONTRIBUTORS

KATIE FRUGÉ is a stomach cancer survivor, special-needs parent, amateur baker, professional theologian, and human rights advocate. She has a PhD in systematic theology, her primary area of interest is the *imago Dei* and human dignity. She serves as director for the Center for Cultural Engagement and Christian Life Commission of the Baptist General Convention of Texas.

GRANT GAINES along with his wife Melisa and their five children, lives in Murfreesboro, Tennessee where he serves as senior pastor of Belle Aire Baptist Church. He holds a PhD in systematic theology from the Southern Baptist Theological Seminary in Louisville, Kentucky, and along with pastoring has taught undergraduate and masters level courses in the Bible and theology.

J. D. GREEAR is the pastor of the Summit Church in Raleigh-Durham, North Carolina and has authored several books, including *What Are You Going to Do with Your Life?* (2020), *Searching for Christmas (2020), Above All* (2019), *Not God Enough* (2018), and *Gaining by Losing* (2015). He completed his PhD in theology at the Southeastern Baptist Theological Seminary. He served as the sixty-second president of the Southern Baptist Convention. Pastor J. D. and his wife Veronica are raising four awesome kids: Kharis, Alethia, Ryah, and Adon.

DEAN INSERRA is a graduate of Liberty University and holds a MA in theological studies from Midwestern Baptist Theological Seminary. He is the founding pastor of City Church. Dean is passionate about reaching the city of Tallahassee with the gospel, to see a worldwide impact made for Jesus. He is married to Krissie and they have two sons, Tommy and Ty, and one daughter, Sally Ashlyn.

CHRIS MARTIN is an editor at Moody Publishers and author of *Terms of Service: The Real Cost of Social Media* (2022), and *The Wolf in Their Pockets: 12 Ways the Social Internet Threatens the People You Lead* (2023). He lives outside Nashville, Tennessee with his family.

BRETT MCCRACKEN is a senior editor and director of communications at the Gospel Coalition. He is the author of *The Wisdom Pyramid: Feeding Your Soul in a Post-Truth World* (2021), *Uncomfortable: The Awkward and Essential Challenge of Christian Community* (2017), *Gray Matters: Navigating the Space Between Legalism and Liberty* (2013), and *Hipster Christianity: When Church and Cool Collide* (2010). Brett and his wife, Kira, live in Santa Ana, California, with their three children. They belong to Southlands Church, and Brett serves as an elder.

KEITH PLUMMER holds a PhD from Trinity Evangelical Divnity School and is the dean of the School of Divinity and a professor of theology at Cairn University in Langhorne, Pennsylvania. He previously served as a pastor in the Evangelical Free Church of America. He and his wife, Ingrid, have two adult children.

JUAN SÁNCHEZ holds a PhD from the Southern Baptist Theological Seminary and serves as senior pastor of High Pointe Baptist Church. He is the author of numerous books, his most recent being *The Leadership Formula: Develop the Next Generation of Leaders in the Church* (2020). Juan has been married to Jeanine since 1990, and they have five adult daughters.

SARAH EEKHOFF ZYLSTRA is senior writer and faith-and-work editor for the Gospel Coalition. She is also the coauthor of *Gospelbound: Living with Resolute Hope in an Anxious Age* (2021) and editor of *Social Sanity in an Insta World* (2022). She earned a BA in english and communication from Dordt University and an MSJ from Medill School of Journalism at Northwestern University. She lives with her husband and two sons in the suburbs of Chicago.

HOW TO USE THIS STUDY

This Bible study provides a guided process for individuals and small groups to explore how our digital age is shaping and forming us and to understand how to live as faithful Christians in a time where technology consumes more and more of our time. Six weeks of study examine different facets of following Jesus in a digital age:

1. TECHNOLOGY AND THE BIBLE

2. DISCIPLESHIP

3. IDENTITY

4. TRUTH

5. RELATIONSHIPS

6. WISDOM

Each week has a group study as well as three personal studies.

GROUP STUDY

Six group sessions are provided that are designed to spark gospel conversations around brief video teachings. Each group session is divided into four sections:

1. START focuses participants on the topic of the session's teaching.

2. WATCH provides space to take notes.

3. DISCUSS guides the group to examine and understand the video teaching and the week's topic.

4. PRAYER closes the group by connecting with God and thanking Him for what we've shared.

PERSONAL STUDY

One week of Bible study is devoted to each of these topics, and each week is divided into three sections of personal study. In these sections you'll find biblical teaching and interactive questions that will help you understand and apply the teaching.

1. LEARN connects the week's topic to the text of the Bible and guides us to rethink how we engage with technology.

2. INFLUENCE asks us to evaluate the areas in life where we have or exert influence and challenges us to make the most of those opportunities.

3. PRACTICE gives us practical handles to interact wisely with the technology and devices around us.

LEADER GUIDE

If you're leading a group through this content, there is a guide in the back to help you lead the group portion of the study.

Week 1

TECHNOLOGY AND THE BIBLE

» START

Use this section to get the conversation going.

■ **Share one piece of technology that you would say is integral to your life.**

Some of us never think about our technology habits until we have a problem we can't seem to fix or something isn't working the way it's supposed to work. And as technology has become integrated into every aspect of our lives, many are starting to question what role these tools should play and what they may be doing to us given how we are constantly connected to our smartphones and devices.

■ **Why do you think many Christians don't consider how their faith informs the technology they use or don't use?**

One of the biggest temptations in the digital age for Christians is to think that our faith doesn't address the pressing questions of technology we face today. Since we can't find smartphones, algorithms, or social media in the back of our Bible, we might mistakenly believe that the Bible doesn't offer us any wisdom about how to interact with ideas and devices that weren't invented when the Bible was written.

One of the biggest reasons we often fail to see how the Bible addresses technology is that we focus on technology as simply a tool we use rather than seeing the distinct ways technology is shaping us that are often contrary to our faith. So at the beginning of our time together we're going to ask and answer some questions to get us on the same page and set the course for the rest of our study.

» WATCH

Use this space to take notes during the video.

» DISCUSS

I. WHAT IS TECHNOLOGY?

■ **How would you define technology?**

Trying to define technology can seem like a tall order, but at the same time something so simple that we just assume we know the answer. We tend to think of technology as simply the internet, our smartphones, various gadgets, or even social media. But if you take a minute to think about those answers, you'll realize that those are simply forms of digital technology and that humanity has always had some form of technology—whether it be a shovel, medicine, or the printing press. Technology has been with us from the very beginning. A better way to define technology is to say that:

> *Technology is a tool, but one that is shaping us*
> *in distinct ways as part of a larger culture.*

■ **What are some "distinct ways" technology is shaping you?**

2. IS TECHNOLOGY GOOD, BAD, OR NEUTRAL?

■ **Take a moment to list out four different forms of technology and try to decide if they are essentially good, bad, or morally neutral. Once you've listed them compare your answers with the group.**

FOLLOWING JESUS IN A DIGITAL AGE

You likely weren't able to come to a consensus on these labels because of how complex technology really is. The same tool can be used in ways that are God-honoring and in ways that are dangerous. Technology is not really good, bad, or neutral, but it is deeply shaping us—including how we see God, ourselves, and the world around us.

3. HOW MIGHT TECHNOLOGY BE SHAPING YOU IN BOTH GODLY AND UNGODLY WAYS?

■ **What is a way technology is shaping you to be more like Christ?**

What is a way that technology is shaping you in ungodly ways?

Throughout this study we'll be considering this question in more detail. Technology is a tool but one that is shaping us in distinct ways (week 2). It is altering how we perceive our identity as human beings in relation to God and our neighbors (week 3), how we perceive what is true and good (week 4), and even how we communicate with one another (week 5). How is it possible that the same tool can affect people in such drastically different ways? And how do we go about cultivating wisdom for the digital age (week 6)?

4. WHAT DOES THE BIBLE SAY ABOUT TECHNOLOGY?

■ **What are some stories or passages of Scripture that shed light on the power of technology to form or shape how we perceive the world?**

List some passages where humanity used our creative and tool-making gifts to make a name for ourselves rather than worship God.

5. HOW HAS GOD CALLED HIS PEOPLE TO LIVE IN LIGHT OF THE GIFTS HE HAS GIVEN US?

■ **Read Deuteronomy 6:4-7 and Matthew 22:37-39.**

What do these passages teach us about how to use the technological and creative gifts God has given us?

PRAYER

Lord, You are the creator of everything and You are in control of everything, including the technologies we make and use. We ask that You give us wisdom in thinking about technology and how we can use it in ways that honor You. Help us to see that technology is shaping us in ways often contrary to our faith and help us to consider Your glory above our own interests when navigating the wild world of technology today. In Jesus's name, amen.

Personal Study 1
LEARN

WHAT DOES THE BIBLE TEACH ABOUT TECHNOLOGY?

In the group session, we briefly introduced and began to answer the question: What does the Bible teach about technology? Yet as we begin to answer, we also recognize that for many of us, even though we believe the Bible teaches us what to believe and how to act, we believe it doesn't offer much guidance about many of the questions we face today like those related to technology.

■ **What questions do you have about the Bible and technology that you hope to see answered in this study?**

We saw that the Bible teaches us that technology is a tool, but one that is shaping us in distinct ways. Let's try and develop this idea and see what God's Word says about the nature of technology and how it is shaping us.

While there is not a letter from the apostle Paul or a warning from one of the prophets about social media, smartphones, or artificial intelligence, Scripture offers principles and practices that should characterize the Christian life no matter the challenges we face. Many of these principles apply to the way Christians should think about and engage with the gift of technology. Let's turn to Exodus 31–32—a text that reminds us of God's good gifts and how we often abuse them to build ourselves up rather than honor God:

> The LORD also spoke to Moses: "Look, I have appointed by name Bezalel son of Uri, son of Hur, of the tribe of Judah. I have filled him with God's Spirit, with wisdom, understanding, and ability in every craft to design artistic works in gold, silver, and bronze, to cut gemstones for mounting, and to carve wood for work in every craft. I have also selected Oholiab

son of Ahisamach, of the tribe of Dan, to be with him. I have put wisdom in the heart of every skilled artisan in order to make all that I have commanded you: the tent of meeting, the ark of the testimony, the mercy seat that is on top of it, and all the other furnishings of the tent— the table with its utensils, the pure gold lampstand with all its utensils, the altar of incense, the altar of burnt offering with all its utensils, the basin with its stand—the specially woven garments, both the holy garments for the priest Aaron and the garments for his sons to serve as priests, the anointing oil, and the fragrant incense for the sanctuary. They must make them according to all that I have commanded you."
EXODUS 31:1-11

■ **What gifts from God did you notice in this passage? How are these creative gifts related to our use of technology?**

Exodus tells us that the Lord filled a man (Bezalel) with God's spirit, wisdom, understanding, and ability in every craft to design and create things for God's glory and for the good of the people. Those abilities were good and were given to all the craftsmen of the day to create what God had commanded them. God used these gifts to build different articles and elements for a place of worship where He would be able to dwell in Israel—the tabernacle.

WHY DID GOD GIVE THESE GIFTS TO MEN?

When God commands us to do something, it is for our benefit that we do it. God knows what is good for us because He created us and cares deeply for us, including the things we use our God-given skills and talents to make. God delights when we use our gifts to bring Him glory. But if you know the story, you know that these abilities and tools were misused and abused by a sinful people.

Look at Exodus 32:1-10:

When the people saw that Moses delayed in coming down from the mountain, they gathered around Aaron and said to him, "Come, make gods for us who will go before us because this Moses, the man who brought us up from the land of Egypt—we don't know what has happened to him!"

Aaron replied to them, "Take off the gold rings that are on the ears of your wives, your sons, and your daughters and bring them to me." So all the people took off the gold rings that were on their ears and brought them to Aaron. He took the gold from them, fashioned it with an engraving tool, and made it into an image of a calf.

Then they said, "Israel, these are your gods, who brought you up from the land of Egypt!"

When Aaron saw this, he built an altar in front of it and made an announcement: "There will be a festival to the LORD tomorrow." Early the next morning they arose, offered burnt offerings, and presented fellowship offerings. The people sat down to eat and drink, and got up to party.

The LORD spoke to Moses: "Go down at once! For your people you brought up from the land of Egypt have acted corruptly. They have quickly turned from the way I commanded them; they have made for themselves an image of a calf. They have bowed down to it, sacrificed to it, and said, 'Israel, these are your gods, who brought you up from the land of Egypt.'"

The LORD also said to Moses, "I have seen this people, and they are indeed a stiff-necked people. Now leave me alone, so that my anger can burn against them and I can destroy them. Then I will make you into a great nation."

EXODUS 32:1-10

■ **How were the gifts given in this passage used for sinful purposes?**

Almost immediately, God's people went from hearing His instructions about creating a place of worship to using their gifts to create a false image of worship. They sought to make a name for themselves similar to the Tower of Babel (Genesis 11) rather than honoring God. As a result, the Lord's anger burned against them because they had used the gifts He gave them to worship Him in order to worship other gods. Ultimately, they put themselves in the place of God by disobeying His commands. The tools and abilities they were given for righteous purposes were used instead to rebel against God and His desire to dwell among His people.

■ **Review your answers from the previous two questions. What can you learn about how to use the gifts of technology from these passages?**

Based on these stories, how might Christians connect to God's intent to how we use our technologies and talents to love God and others?

While some may see the Bible as an ancient document that is unconcerned with contemporary questions of technology, it is clear that the gift to envision and create technology comes from God. He has given us gifts and has instilled in us the ability to create these tools, but we routinely use these gifts to honor ourselves rather than to honor and worship Him.

Our creative gifts along with our sinful heart can be a recipe for disaster unless we take the time to slow down and ask the hard questions about what technology is and how it is shaping us. We need God's help.

In Exodus 32:10, despite the corruption of Israel and their worship of idols, God promised them that He would make Israel into a great nation. While our technologies and tools may disciple us in ways that take emphasis off God and put it on ourselves, God's plan for us and our technology is never thwarted. God's plan is not only good but is unchangeable.

Personal Study 2
INFLUENCE

THE GLORY OF GOD AND THE GOOD OF OTHERS

In our digital age, it is increasingly evident that we are easily distracted and inclined to use our God-given gifts such as technology in ways that don't bring glory to God. While this might seem like a new problem, the previous personal study demonstrated that it is an age-old problem. If that's the case, how does the Bible instruct us to use our gifts and talents—and even our technology—to love God?

The Great Commandment is the perfect place for instruction because here Jesus sums up the entirety of how Christians are called to live in light of God's truths.

> *When the Pharisees heard that he had silenced the Sadducees, they came together. And one of them, an expert in the law, asked a question to test him: "Teacher, which command in the law is the greatest?"*
>
> *He said to him, "Love the Lord your God with all your heart, with all your soul, and with all your mind. This is the greatest and most important command. The second is like it: Love your neighbor as yourself. All the Law and the Prophets depend on these two commands."*
> **MATTHEW 22:34-40**

Jesus summarized the entirety of the Christian life—loving God and loving others. Notice how Jesus's command directs us outside of ourselves. Instead of focusing on what we might want or making it all about us, He points to others.

Think about all the different areas of life you're actively involved in. Take me for example: I am a husband and a father to two boys, a son, a brother, a church member, an ethicist and instructor at a Christian college, and a writer! In each of these areas of life, I have duties and responsibilities to other people. God has placed me in these contexts and calls me to live above reproach and walk in wisdom as I seek to love him and love those around me (Ephesians 5:15; 1 Peter 2:9).

Given how technology has been incorporated into nearly every area of our lives, from our personal life to our families, our work, and even our churches, we must think wisely and biblically about how these tools are shaping and forming us. We'll dive deeper into this concept of how technology is discipling us in the next session, but we should note here the various areas of life where God is calling us to follow Him by loving Him and our neighbor. The command to love God and love our neighbor extends to every area of our lives, include how we use the technologies that God has given us.

Technology is something that we incorporate into the different areas of our lives to make things run simply and more efficiently. That's one of the main goals of technology—by design it is intended to make things easier and more streamlined. It can obviously make our lives easier and more convenient but we must not forget its true purpose and power.

As we think about the spheres of influence we find ourselves in, let's start in the middle and work our way out.

■ **First, how might you use technology as an individual to love God with you whole heart? Soul? Mind?**

Second, how might you use technology to love you spouse, family, or roommates better?

Third, how might you use technology to love your neighbors and your church better?

Every one of us has benefited from some sort of technology, and that should be no surprise. God gave us the ability to create these tools; He intended for us to have them. The point of this study is to help all of us think wisely about how we use these innovative tools so that we use them to love God and our neighbor well.

Personal Study 3
PRACTICE

IDENTIFYING HABITS

We know that in most things, breaking bad habits takes a while and is not easy, because habits form over time. Without realizing it, you've likely developed various habits with technology that radically alter how you interact with the world around you.

What is your morning routine like? I imagine that you likely have a very similar routine to me. Each morning, I instinctively reach for my phone the moment I wake up, usually by my alarm (or more often lately by our two sons who have recently become early risers). For some reason, I always expect to see a host of notifications, including little red badges on various apps telling me everything I supposedly missed between last night's final check and this morning's scroll. But there is nothing of note outside a few email newsletters, which are often news-related, to start the day and an increasingly long to-do list that I never seem to get caught up on. Almost without thinking before getting out of bed, I make my rounds through various apps on my phone. I check my email, my social media feeds, and various work tools, to see what I might have missed overnight. I do all of this without even realizing that apart from my overseas friends, most of the folks I know have been sleeping. But something seems to push me to check all of these things before I even put my feet on the floor.

This constant push to check our devices and apps is one of the countless ways technology is shaping and forming us. There are some important questions to ask ourselves when trying to address how to better use technology for good purposes.

These questions easily apply to any technology. But for the sake of today's exercise, identify one piece of technology you use and consider the answers to these questions.

■ **Why do you use this particular form of technology?**

Are you using these tools primarily to love God and love others or to make a name for yourself? This can be one of the most eye-opening questions.

In what contexts and at what times are you drawn to your devices or social media? Is there a pattern that emerges?

Is it hard for you to go long periods of time without your devices or social media? If so, why?

How is your technology use negatively influencing other habits or affecting your relationships with your spouse, roommate, kids, small group, pastor, or neighbors?

If we can answer these questions truthfully and honestly, then we have a good foundation for thinking about new ways to use different technology in our lives and how we can redeem our time while using it. In the next session, we will explore more about how technology is discipling us and shaping how we see others and the world around us.

Week 2

DISCIPLESHIP

» START

Use this section to get the conversation going.

As we discussed in the last session, technology is not simply a tool that we use but something that is shaping us in profound ways as we use it. So far, we have begun to explore how it is altering how we see God, ourselves, and even the world around us. It can change how we see our neighbors and how we interact with others in our families, church, school, and office. We are all being discipled by something, and technology is one of the most formative tools in our lives.

■ **How often do you check notifications on devices throughout the day? Is this something you wish you did less? Explain.**

What are some ways technology has altered the habits and rhythms of your life? How has it shaped you in ways that are similar to diet, exercise, or even spiritual habits?

If we take an honest assessment of our habits with technology, we'll quickly see the ways it's altering how we perceive our identity as human beings in relation to God and our neighbors. We start to see other people as a means to an end, bits of data, or opponents in online debates rather than people worthy of dignity and respect.

Whether we're consciously aware of them or not, we've all felt the reorienting effect technology has on our lives. So, what are we to do about it? Is there any hope for us to turn the tables in this push by technology toward convenience and efficiency? That's what we're going to be considering today.

» WATCH

Use this space to take notes during the video.

» DISCUSS

Discipleship is a crucial aspect of the Christian life. Jesus commanded His followers to "make disciples" (Matthew 28:19-20). Discipleship is essential to the mission of God, but discipleship isn't just sharing the gospel message with others. True discipleship requires reorienting and reshaping our entire lives. It alters how we think, how we act, how we engage with others, and how we love God and our neighbors.

Just by doing a study like this you are being discipled, as we talk about the Bible, technology, and the Christian life. But what about that device that never leaves your side? How is it discipling you? We have become so enamored with our technology and tools that we fail to see that these tools are reshaping everything about us, often in ways that are not in line with our faith. But let's first start by defining discipleship and why it is central to the Christian life.

■ **Read Matthew 22:37-39 and Matthew 28:19-20.**

  How should the instruction to love God and love our neighbors affect the way we seek to make disciples?

  What are some ways our technology use helps or hurts our ability to follow these two commands?

The commands of Jesus are dependent upon one another and meant to be obeyed simultaneously. We can't separate the command to love God and others from the command to make disciples. Additionally, we cannot separate the way we use technology from these clear commands of Christ. All that we do as Christians should be done to the glory of God—including how we use technology.

■ **Read Galatians 5:22-25.**

Galatians 5 describes the fruit of the Spirit, which are qualities given to every believer by the Holy Spirit.

■ **Consider someone you know who often embodies the fruit of the Spirit. What kinds of habits and practices in his or her life demonstrate the work of the Spirit?**

We are always being discipled by something (see Romans 12:2). We are always being formed and shaped by the things we do and the things we are exposed to. Just as technology shapes us in particular ways, our habits push us in a particular direction. With that in mind, let's evaluate our habits and how they're shaping us. Don't feel guilty about your answers. Part of recognizing the things that shape us is taking an honest assessment of our lives and habits.

■ **Write down how often you read God's word, pray, attend church gatherings, small groups, and so forth throughout a week.**

Now write down how long you think you spend on your devices.

Compare your usage and time spent in these two areas. What encourages you and what might be convicting you right now? Discuss with your group.

How are your technology habits making you more loving, joyful, peaceful, patient, kind, oriented toward goodness, faithful, gentle, and self-controlled?

How might you better align your technology habits with the biblical vision of discipleship?

PRAYER

Lord, You are the creator of all things and for each gift we are blessed with, we give thanks to You for it. Help us to remember that we live in a sinful, fallen world and if we are not being formed by Your Word, we will be formed by the world and the things in it. Let us be more prayerful in the way we engage with the world, seeking to be wise in what we expose ourselves to each day. With technology, help us to disciple others in how to use it for Your glory rather than simply being used and formed by it. You are sovereign over everything and that includes every aspect of the digital world. In Jesus's name, amen.

Personal Study 1
LEARN

Think back to our definition of technology:

Technology is a tool, but one that is shaping us
in distinct ways as part of a larger culture.

So far in our study we have discussed how technology is a tool that is shaping (discipling) us in particular ways that are often at odds with the biblical vision of discipleship.

The biblical vision of discipleship is to become more like Christ as we exhibit the fruits of the Spirit as seen in Galatians 5:22-25. The question we must ask ourselves is if our technology habits are encouraging or discouraging us from living out spiritual fruit such as "love, joy, peace, patience, kindness, goodness, faithfulness, gentleness, and self-control" from the place of a renewed heart and mind.

Part of understanding how our digital age shapes our discipleship is seeing how technology operates inside a larger cultural context. In our definition of technology, the last part focuses on the idea that technology is "part of a larger culture." So what does that really mean?

■ **Where have you seen a tool or piece of technology influence our broader culture?**

TECHNOLOGY AS PART OF A LARGER CULTURE

Let's think about this question by examining an increasingly common device in our homes: the smart doorbell. My wife and I love our video doorbell, especially when we are traveling, or someone comes to our door unexpectedly. Not only can we see who is there or when packages arrive (especially when I order more books, to my wife's disdain), but we can also turn off the ringer when our kids are napping and even check on our house when we are out of town.

As I write this, I am traveling and just received a notification that there was a person at our front door even though I am across the country. If we isolate this smart doorbell from the cultural context we inhabit, it may seem that this tool is a nice convenience and doesn't really pose any real dangers or wouldn't be altering my behavior in any significant way.

But stepping back and viewing this common technology through the broader understanding of technology that we have been discussing so far, we can see this innovation is much more than an isolated gadget. It was developed to meet a need brought on by another innovation that came before it—online shopping.

Think about it—we live in a day where more and more of our household needs are delivered right to our front doors through online shopping. Video door-bells are an innovation in response to issues that arose from another innovation. While convenient, the increase in online shopping brought an increase in other issues as well.

After all, that is a lot of delivery people at your house on any given day—people you don't know. And the delivery people aren't the only thing to think about; what about those "porch pirates" who steal packages from doorsteps (especially during the holidays)? Clearly, the smart doorbell wasn't created in a vacuum. It was created to meet a growing concern over home safety from our modern-day package delivery phenomenon. Doorbell technologies also helped to address homeowners' fear of break-ins and satisfied their curiosity of who is around their home even if they live in relatively safe areas. And, in turn, these same cameras also brought about a number of new concerns over neighborhood surveillance and personal privacy. And that's just one example. Most innovations you and I enjoy today are built to solve problems with the innovations that came before them.

■ **Where else have you seen a new technology fix a problem brought about by a previous innovation?**

When we examine a particular form of technology, we need to understand these tools do not exist in isolation. As we zoom out and see the various aspects of the technology web, we see they exist in a larger framework or movement of technology. This means that simple answers or trite platitudes about "reining in screen time" are rarely going to alter our deeply embedded relationship with technology. Instead of just more tips and tricks, we need true biblical wisdom for the digital age.

We must be eyes-wide-open about what we're actually dealing with when it comes to technology—and it's not just a social media platform that distracts us from our work or a phone that takes our attention from our kids. It's not just a doorbell camera or a gadget that makes our life a little more convenient. It's a whole way we've been trained, a whole orientation we walk in, a whole web of relations that does nothing but breed a need to go faster and faster—all built to remove any trace of inefficiency, difficulty, obstacles, or friction in our life.

Technology reminds us that we are all constantly being discipled, being encouraged to respond to the world around us by the tools we use. But how might our technologies be shaping us in ways that are contrary to our faith and contrary to the fruits that Christ followers are to exhibit?

Let's look at Luke 14: 25-27 and 33 for some wisdom on discipleship.

> *Now great crowds were traveling with [Jesus]. So he turned and said to them, "If anyone comes to me and does not hate his own father and mother, wife and children, brothers and sisters— yes, and even his own life—he cannot be my disciple. Whoever does not bear his own cross and come after me cannot be my disciple . . . In the same way, therefore, every one of you who does not renounce all his possessions cannot be my disciple."*
> **LUKE 14:25-27,33**

■ **How would you summarize what Jesus is saying here?**

This can seem like one of the hardest passages in the Gospels to fully comprehend, since Christ is calling those who follow him to do some pretty radical things. But this type of sacrifice isn't about turning away from your family or abandoning your responsibilities. It is rather a call to a type of discipleship that puts Christ above all earthly things—even our families, jobs, and yes even our habits with technology.

It might sound odd that we are to turn everything over to God in order to be His disciple. One of the reasons for this is that our culture—both non-Christian and even at times our Christian culture—tells us a lie that our life is our own and that what is most important in life is that we are happy and get to decide what is good for us. We've become so saturated in this sense of individualism that we often can't separate this modern belief from our reading of God's Word. We falsely believe that we deserve certain things—especially in light of social media and the internet, which personalize and curate our own online worlds. Technology adapts to our desires and seeks to give us more of what we want.

> ■ **How does following Jesus lead Christians to pursue a radically different life than the one described above?**

TRUE DISCIPLESHIP

But Christian discipleship isn't about indulging in our desires or being able to define our own realities, it's about sacrificing everything in order to pursue Christ above all. Technology subtly alters how we perceive truth, responsibility, and our identity because technology operates inside a larger culture of individualism that takes the focus off God and centers it on us. For all of the good that technology can do in our lives, it often pushes us to see ourselves as the center of the universe.

The calls to "love the Lord your God with all your heart, with all your soul, and with all your mind" and to "love your neighbor as yourself" lead us to an outward-focused love that is not centered on ourselves. Jesus calls us to look outside of ourselves in a culture determined to make life all about us.

■ **How does your technology use encourage you to focus on yourself rather than on God and others?**

How has social media changed—for good and ill—how the church seeks to make disciples of Jesus?

What principles should be kept in mind as we seek to use technology in our families and churches in a loving way towards God and others?

What behavioral or emotional changes have you noticed in yourself and others that have resulted from technology use?

Today, technology has become so prevalent that many of us spend the majority of our time on it for work, school, and leisure without ever thinking twice. As we begin to evaluate technology through this broader lens that we have been discussing, the questions we ask shift from how we can spend less time with/on technology to how we might use technology without letting it be the main forming presence in our lives and if it is wise for us to use these tools. The most important question we can ask in all of life as a disciple of Christ is not, *Can* we do this? But, *Should* we do this? Asking these simple questions puts us on the path to handling complex questions with Christlike wisdom.

CALLED BY HIS OWN GLORY AND GOODNESS

Let's conclude with some wisdom from the apostle Peter about what it means to be a disciple:

> *[God's] divine power has given us everything required for life and godliness through the knowledge of him who called us by his own glory and goodness. By these he has given us very great and precious promises, so that through them you may share in the divine nature, escaping the corruption that is in the world because of evil desire. For this very reason, make every effort to supplement your faith with goodness, goodness with knowledge, knowledge with self-control, self-control with endurance, endurance with godliness, godliness with brotherly affection, and brotherly affection with love. For if you possess these qualities in increasing measure, they will keep you from being useless or unfruitful in the knowledge of our Lord Jesus Christ.*
> **2 PETER 1:3-8**

In a world where so many other things are competing to disciple you, we must prioritize our relationship with the Lord. As we press into Him, we're able to receive everything needed to be His disciples ("called...[for] his own glory and goodness"). It is then through the promises of God that we have hope. That hope is our motivation for resisting the temptation to believe and live according to the other competing narratives trying to disciple us. Christians can live faithfully in the digital age without being a product of the digital age.

Personal Study 2
INFLUENCE

SETTING BOUNDARIES

Most of us use technology in every area of life today, from our school, home, office, car, and even bedroom. We are enamored with technology, and it has become a mainstay in our lives in helpful and harmful ways. Some of us are so connected that we don't have the luxury of being able to make a living or keep tabs on the things we need to without using some form of technology. Even among children, the demand for a smartphone—to watch television, play video games, and use social media apps like Instagram™ and TikTok™—is becoming more and more common to a point where many parents give in at increasingly younger ages. These devices demand our attention and seem to be constantly pulling us in. If we are not careful, we may give our attention and time to them without knowing all that they are doing to us.

Often when we think about technology in the church, we see it simply as a neutral tool that we just use in good or bad ways, instead of seeing how it is shaping us/discipling us in unique ways. In recent years we have even seen that many of the most popular social media accounts for Christians weren't even run by believers but were rather controlled by international bot farms, who are known for flaming the tensions in society and causing unrest.[1]

■ **How does being constantly tied to our devices negatively affect Christians in particular?**

It's important to consider how our habits affect other people as well. You might find that in thinking about your patterns and habits with technology that there are some concerning ones you have formed without recognizing it. Technology isn't only affecting us on the outside; it alters the way we feel about ourselves, the world around us, and towards others.

■ **Does technology cause you to be more hopeful about life or does it stir more anxiety and fear? How so?**

How has technology changed the way you think about and engage with others both in person and online?

Ask a close friend or your spouse to give you an honest assessment of how you act in person vs. online. Do you exhibit the fruit of the Spirit in both settings or do you tend to interact with and treat other people differently online than you would in person?

It is far too easy for all of us to interact with others online in ways that we would never act in person. Among the many ways that technology disciples us is that it seems to encourage us to see people are mere avatars or bits of data rather than people created in the image of God. In our digital age, we routinely act as if someone's value and worth is only tied to their political, social, or religious opinions. We treat others as an enemy to vanquish, rather than a neighbor we are to love and serve. The commandments of Jesus should be obeyed in our online interactions just as much as in person.

■ **How would your online interactions change if you were committed to loving God and others through every virtual exchange?**

Personal Study 3
PRACTICE

While it is important to consider the way we think about technology and how it might be discipling us in ways contrary to the Lord, if our habits and actions don't follow suit, we will always use technology in some unhelpful and ungodly ways. No amount of study, checklists, or questions will free us to be perfect in how we use these tools and how we interact with others.

How we use tools like technology and social media should reflect who we worship. Take some time to fill out the following lists. In the left-hand column note all of the various technologies you use each day from devices to apps and even websites. In the right-hand column write down one good way you can use these tools and one personal danger you might encounter. This will be completely unique to you so take you time and think deeply about these questions.

DAILY TECH	The Good	The Bad

■ **How are you using technology to further God's kingdom and love you neighbor?**

Where might you have room to grow?

In what ways is technology and social media tempting you to treat others in ungodly or dehumanizing ways?

What limits/parameters do you need to put on your devices to help flee these sinful temptations? Be practical and specific.

Week 3

IDENTITY

» START

Use this section to get the conversation going.

Last week we talked about how our technology is shaping and forming us. This week we're going to discuss the ways technology is subtly yet radically discipling us to see our identity as something inside of ourselves rather than outside of us and how that leads us to seek approval and validation from those around us, especially on social media.

- **Which social media platform do you enjoy the most and why?**

Do you ever struggle with wanting to portray yourself a certain way online? If so, explain.

Online it is far too easy to give in to the political, social, cultural, or religious polarization or the "us vs. them" of the day. Without intending to, we fall back into focusing on what our "tribe" thinks and how others might view what we say or how we interact online. On top of that, it constantly seems that people are angry with one another and treat others as less than human when they disagree with them.

While we might have the best intentions of modeling Christlikeness in our online interactions, without thinking, our online behavior can become more about being seen as the "right kind of person" or on the "right team." We've all felt this tension. This week we're going to press into the tension as we think about how our digital age forms our identity.

» WATCH

Use this space to take notes during the video.

» DISCUSS

People all over the world are asking themselves the important question, *Who am I?*

■ **If someone asked you to define your identity or who you are, what would you say? It may be easy here to write the "right" answer but think deeply about how you introduce yourself to other people and the way you present yourself online.**

Technology is shaping and forming us in very particular ways as we use it each day, including how we view ourselves as people. A phrase that has taken on more and more meaning in our culture recently is the phrase "identity crisis." While this phrase might take on different meanings depending on the context of its usage, what we mean is that people are questioning who they truly are. We live in a society that is seeking to craft our own identities (online and in person) and then to have those identities validated by those around us. We all desperately want to be seen as the right kind of person in the middle of cultural confusion and tension, as we define our own identities.

■ **What are some of the common ways we describe our identity in our digital age?**

What are some "lesser things" that we allow to define our identity? What draws us to these things?

Online activism is one of many ways we see people forming their identity around lesser things. When a crisis or tragedy happened in the past, it was often discussed in the public square (city halls, school board meetings, newspapers, magazines, local stores, etc.) where people came to address and discuss the issues and a way forward in their local context.

But today, the public square has been exchanged for social media platforms and online forums. People take their activism away from their local context and city square to their devices and apps that have an international reach. If we spend even just a little bit of time on the platforms where conversations like this happen, we can easily see how hostile and uncivilized the conversations are becoming, given our lack of real-life relationships.

■ **When have you seen online activism turn into a shouting match? What does that reveal about the way we view ourselves in the public square?**

The beliefs we hold are important, and they help express who we are, but every person we meet is far more complex than the sum of his or her beliefs. His or her value and worth is not rooted simply in what he or she believes on a particular issue but in whose image he or she has been created. Value, worth, and identity are given to us by God.

■ **Invite a few volunteers to read Genesis 1:26-28, Romans 8:29, Ephesians 4:24, Colossians 3:10, and James 3:9.**

Based on these Scriptures, what does it mean to be made in the image of God?

■ **Why is seeing ourselves and others as being made in the image of God a more reliable and helpful way of viewing ourselves than the image of ourselves we often seek to craft online?**

How does this change the way we participate in the digital public square, especially on social media today?

What is one adjustment you need to make to the way you see or portray yourself or others based on this discussion?

PRAYER

Lord, You are the creator of all things. You made us according to Your very image and You call us to reflect You in every aspect of our lives. Help us to live for You, loving You with everything in us and loving our neighbors as ourselves especially as we engage online. May we become more faithful to Your commands, teachings, and instructions, in everything looking to serve You and others. In Jesus's name, amen.

Personal Study 1
LEARN

IN HIS IMAGE FROM THE BEGINNING

We know from the very beginning of Scripture that God created all humans with inherent value and dignity because we are all made in the image of God (Genesis 1:26-28). But because of the fall and our rebellion, every human is a sinner and in need of the saving work of Jesus (Romans 3:23). Jesus came into the world, fully God and fully man, and was crucified, buried, and resurrected. Through this He atoned for our sins and offers eternal life to all those who believe, repent, and call upon His name. He restored our relationship with God and made us a new creation with a new identity rooted in Himself, who is the true Image of God (Colossians 1:15).

But even as those who trust in Christ for salvation and are given a new identity, we continually fall short of living perfectly righteous lives before God (Romans 5:8). We don't always perfectly live out our true identity in Christ. As we have already discussed, our identity in Christ consists not only of having the right beliefs but also the right actions. True belief alters our actions, and our actions reveal what we truly believe. We are called to be consistent in both word and deed, and to always reflect Christ—no matter whether it's to the person down the street or to the person commenting on our feeds.

■ **How has following Jesus shaped the way you view your identity?**

So, where have we gone wrong? Where have we missed the mark? Let's look at a passage in the Gospel of Mark, where Jesus showed His disciples what this identity meant and how it changed everything about their lives.

IDENTITY THROUGH DENIAL

Calling the crowd along with his disciples, he said to them, "If anyone wants to follow after me, let him deny himself, take up his cross, and follow me. For whoever wants to save his life will lose it, but whoever loses his life because of me and the gospel will save it. For what does it benefit someone to gain the whole world and yet lose his life? What can anyone give in exchange for his life? For whoever is ashamed of me and my words in this adulterous and sinful generation, the Son of Man will also be ashamed of him when he comes in the glory of his Father with the holy angels."
MARK 8:34-38

Jesus addressed both the crowds and His disciples, telling them that if they wished to be His followers, ambassadors for the kingdom, that their lives should look different from the rest of the world. Their beliefs and knowledge must be reflected in their actions. Everything about their lives is to be different because of who they are following.

■ **In light of Mark 8:34-38, make two lists in the columns below:**

Characteristics that define a disciple of Christ	Characteristics that define the world

Based off of these lists, try to apply some of those ideas to what it may look like to follow Jesus in our digital age. Think about Romans 12:2 for some help.

> *Do not be conformed to this age, but be transformed*
> *by the renewing of your mind, so that you may discern*
> *what is the good, pleasing, and perfect will of God.*
> **ROMANS 12:2**

■ **What might it look like for someone to follow Jesus today instead of being conformed to this world?**

God's Word transcends time and place and applies to our digital culture. Specifically, it applies to how our identity in Christ conflicts with some of the competing cultural identities we are exposed to each day in our digital lives. Whereas consumption and crafting our own identities has become the priority in our digital age, for the Christian the outlook on life is completely different. We have a secure identity in Christ as we follow Him, thus our lives (and our social media feeds) should look radically different from the rest of the world.

It would be naïve to say that this is an easy task or a quick fix. But understanding who we are, what we were made for, and how we are to live in light of those things, is essential to living faithfully as Christ followers in this digital age, and in any age for that matter.

One of the most important aspects of living in a digital culture is how easy it is to group ourselves together into certain groups based on politics, culture, preferences, and a host of other things. It quickly becomes "us vs. them" as we isolate ourselves into our comfortable groupings online and in person.

Most of us experience this when a breaking news story takes place, or some major social or political event happens. Within moments, battle lines are drawn and sides are taken. Our timelines are full of hot takes and soapboxes as everyone tries to be the first to say just the right thing and to identify themselves as the "right kind of person." Everyone takes sides in the debate within moments (often before the full story and context is even known) and puts on their team's colors. Someone often posts something slightly inflammatory about the other side and then everyone piles on in order to be seen by their own side. Then the cycle repeats.

■ **What is it about social media and technology today that tends to separate us into rivaling teams and pushes us to draw battle lines?**

What is behind this growing polarization and temptation for each of us to define our identity by which team we are on rather than in Christ?

One downside of our digital age is the tendency to feel like all of this division and discord is new. Paul recognized these sort of tensions and divisions in his letter to the church of Galatia well before our digital age.

> *For you were called to be free, brothers and sisters; only don't use this freedom as an opportunity for the flesh, but serve one another through love. For the whole law is fulfilled in one statement: Love your neighbor as yourself. But if you bite and devour one another, watch out, or you will be consumed by one another.*
> **GALATIANS 5:13-15**

True freedom, purpose, and identity—what our friends and neighbors so desperately long for—is only found in God. He created us, knows the most intimate details of our lives, and what we most long for today.

■ **How does the gospel transcend your tribal identities and groupings, especially online?**

What does it look like to "love your neighbor as yourself" in your online discourse?

What does it look like to "love your [online] neighbor as yourself" when they aren't showing that same love and honor to you?

Our words and deeds must reflect the way we answer the important question, *Who am I?* In fact, our words and actions will reflect our identity and who we truly worship—whether that is God or ourselves. End dwelling on these things in Paul's letter to the Colossians, aligning your head, heart, and hands with them, to go out and live in Christ and for Christ in the digital age.

Devote yourselves to prayer; stay alert in it with thanksgiving. At the same time, pray also for us that God may open a door to us for the word, to speak the mystery of Christ, for which I am in chains, so that I may make it known as I should. Act wisely toward outsiders, making the most of the time. Let your speech always be gracious, seasoned with salt, so that you may know how you should answer each person.
COLOSSIANS 4:2-6

Personal Study 2
INFLUENCE

CHRISTIAN IDENTITY IS NOT COMPARTMENTALIZED

We have seen that these various roles or spheres of influence that we operate in cause us to ask different questions about what it means to be a follower of Jesus in the digital age. If we are not careful though, we can easily fall victim to compartmentalizing our Christian identity, especially in light of technologies like social media and digital culture. Our Christian beliefs and actions may be easy to hold together in one sphere (for example, home life or family) yet difficult in another (for example, workplace or social media). The temptation is to simply accept this rather than dwell deeply on why this might be the case and then pray about how to walk in wisdom in every area of life. A common lie we are told is that our "real life" in person is more meaningful than what we do in our "online life." This false belief leads us to think that what happens online isn't real life. Therefore, we're tempted to say things we would never say in person or act in ways that we would be embarrassed to with other people around.

■ **What convictions are you tempted to sideline in your online engagement? Do you act differently on different platforms? For example, "tell it as it is, no matter the cost" on one and "kind, loving, and gracious" on another.**

Do you interact with your friends, family, and colleagues the same way online as you do in person? What about those you disagree with? Explain.

Evaluate who you follow online and see how they interact with others, especially if you are more of an observer online rather than someone who regularly posts on social media. What patterns do you observe in their lives, both good and bad?

How might your interactions (both passive and active) online be inconsistent with your true Christian identity?

One of the many lies we believe about our neighbors is that we must be in a constant battle, an "us vs. them" mentality. We forget or choose not to see others for who they really are: made in the image of God.

■ **What does the "us vs. them" mentality look like in your personal life? Your work? Your friendships?**

It isn't always the popular way to perceive your enemies, especially online, but Christ is clear that we are to love our enemies and treat them with respect even as we disagree with them (Matthew 5:43-44). Love is one of the essential elements of the Christian identity and is the backbone of the Christian life. We should be known in this world for love (John 13:35). We have experienced the love of God and in turn, we get to show it to others.

■ **How might you demonstrate Christlike love online?**

Personal Study 3
PRACTICE

WE ALL SEARCH FOR IDENTITY SOMEWHERE

Our Christian identity alters our thinking as well as our actions. Our beliefs shape our actions and our actions demonstrate our true beliefs. This balance is the essence of how the Bible describes wisdom. Biblical wisdom is essential in Christian discipleship because it helps God's people see how they are to live in light of God's truth. It helps God's people walk God's ways as transformed creatures called to reflect our Creator in the world, whether that be in our families, workplaces, churches, and especially in our personal lives.

Instead of focusing on people "out there," wisdom calls us to ask the hard questions of ourselves and how we each are seeking to craft particular identities in this digital age. While it may be tempting to pass on by this section, I encourage you to push through because this is where the proverbial "rubber meets the road" and is an opportunity for us to apply the things we have been talking about so far.

■ **Think about these identities that we may seek to craft online and circle the one that you think best describes you.[2] After you reflect on this, ask a close friend, spouse, or roommate to do the same for you. Compare your answers.**

IDENTITY I: THE PLATFORM BUILDER/INFLUENCER

It feels good when people start "following" you, share the things you post, or even seek to mimic your lifestyle and the things you recommend. Almost like a drug, it can become addicting as you begin to intentionally seek these things out and rearrange your life for that perfect picture, business sponsorship, or whatever might expand your influence online. Leveraging your influence for good can be God-honoring, but when that influence is used to expand a personal platform or reoriented to serve yourself, it can quickly become an idol.

■ **What needs or desires does the platform builder/influencer have that can only be truly met by Jesus?**

IDENTITY 2: THE CULTURE WARRIOR

You are known more for what you are against than what you are for. Consistently angry tweets, sarcastic put-downs, monologues/rants on Facebook™, and trite videos calling out your "enemies" on TikTok™ are a clear sign that something deep is going on. These types of posts often gain a ton of attention (good and bad), which can encourage the same behaviors over and over again.

It's far too easy online to share information without context in order to be the first one to post, to be bombastic or reactionary in your engagements with others, or to even attack with uncharitable and unkind words, all in order to be seen as the right kind of person. These things will build a platform for being willing to "speak the truth." Of all the identities we seek to craft in the digital age, this one can be tricky, as it is easy to delude ourselves into thinking that we always have righteous motivations to stand for what is right.

■ **What needs or desires does the culture warrior have that can only be truly met by Jesus?**

IDENTITY 3: THE EXPERT

Technology and social media encourages us all to be generalists in the sense that we feel the need to comment or give our opinion on most issues or events. We see the same person pretend to be an expert on medical, legal, theological, and even literary topics all at the same time. Do you do this? Are you quick to weigh in on anything and everything? Maybe it's not anything and everything—maybe it's a particular area of culture you can't hold yourself back from throwing in your two cents. The medical field. The political realm. The education sector. The theological arena. Whatever it is, do you fancy yourself the "well-read person" in the comment section—even if "well-read" only means you scanned a few articles online? If so, process with God why you need to be the expert every time you enter a virtual space.

■ **What needs or desires does the expert have that can only be truly met by Jesus?**

IDENTITY 4: THE PERFECT PARENT

This one can get tricky for a number of reasons. First, it is a righteous and God-honoring desire and calling to seek to train up your children in the way they should go (Proverbs 22:6). This is our responsibility as parents and one that is not to be passed on or given to others. Second, many who fall into this trap initially want to love their kids and even honor the Lord in their parenting. But the "perfect parent" identity can easily be one that takes priority over everything else in life. It can easily become so central that it manifests itself as someone who is always ready to fight with others about what is the best for family life.

One of the quickest and most effective ways to diagnose this unhealthy identity is to ask whether you think you have the best ideas and guidance for your own family or if you think your jurisdiction extends to all others as well. Obviously, you have come to the decisions you have for your own family according to your own convictions, and there's nothing wrong with sharing something that has worked in your family if your peers are asking for help, but if your decisions are somehow always the correct ones for everyone else as well, doesn't that seem a tad ironic and self-serving? What if others felt that way about your kids and mentioned how wrong they thought you were with the ways your lead your own family?

■ **What needs or desires does the perfect parent have that can only be truly met by Jesus?**

IDENTITY 5: THE PASSIVE OBSERVER

You might get to the end of this section and none of these identities are really that big of temptations for you. In many ways that is good news, but one of the subtle and most widespread temptations online is to just be a passive observer of what everyone else is doing online. While you might not be seeking influence or notoriety, we all passively engage on social media at times to blow off some steam, waste some time, or even to avoid doing the hard thing right in front of you. This can be a temptation for all of us (including me). We delude ourselves into thinking we just need to chill out for a bit and passively scroll on social media or otherwise waste time online. While this is not always a bad thing, it can be a dangerous identity when our passive engagement online becomes a way to avoid building relationships, deepen our commitments to God and His church, or even loving our friends and family.

■ **What needs or desires does the passive observer have that can only be truly met by Jesus?**

Which of the identities did you most relate to and why?

Based on a your previous answers, what are a couple of ways you need to rethink your online engagement?

Now that you've pinpointed specific ways you've been building an identity in a certain group—whether it's political or personal or health-related—think about how important conversations in that space have been going over the last few years. Have you all become more joyful, patient, or kind? Could anyone in your group correctly and charitably articulate the viewpoint of those who don't belong in your group, or disagree with it? Has the emotional temperature of the group become more mature and seasoned, or more fiery and combative? Chances are, the environment has grown more combustible over time, not more enlightening or enjoyable.

And, chances are, you are not leaving those environments abounding in the fruit of the Spirit, but rather filled with anxiety, jealousy, anger, pride, or even hatred, which are works of the flesh. This, my friend, is the fruit of crafting identities online uprooted from our true identity in Christ and in our local communities. It is evidence of polarization, and it is why social media is becoming unbearable for many to engage in long-term.

Week 4
TRUTH

» START

Use this section to get the conversation going.

Last week we focused on the crucial issue of identity and saw how the various technologies we engage with alter our view of ourselves.

■ **Take a look at the habits exercise from last week's personal study. Which identity seemed the most like you? How did this exercise challenge you?**

This week we'll be discussing how our digital age shapes how we view and understand truth. We live in an age where breaking news is pushed to our devices through alerts as they happen. It has become common for us to know about something as it is happening, often without context, details, or any real insight into what is really going on. To a degree, these notifications are convenient, the problem with them is that the information is often incomplete or worse, false.

■ **Share about a time when you read a notification, post, or alert and later found out the information you received was wrong, or at best misleading.**

As we've said, technology is discipling us all in very particular ways and forming our view of the world. One of the main ways it does this is by altering how we think about truth and other people. Technology has helped usher in a new culture of suspicion, especially among traditional ways of understanding reality. Truth is becoming something less focused on reality, and instead something simply convenient when it aligns with our cultural, social, or political cause. Our feelings, desires, and personal will have replaced a fixed reality. The very idea of truth is often being eroded right before our eyes.

» WATCH

Use this space to take notes during the video.

» DISCUSS

What is considered true in our society today is in a state of constant flux. What we want to be true often trumps what actually *is* true. Even the idea of truth is a complicated subject in our society today. While pretty much everyone agrees on some basic facts, there is no longer a widespread consensus on some of the most fundamental ideas that our culture is built upon. There is ongoing debate as to whether truth is knowable at all.

■ **What basic truths do you think nearly every person holds to? Do any of these truths transcend the individualism of our day?**

What are some topics where people seem more divided?

We live in an unprecedented age of information, with more than we can even begin to comprehend right at our fingertips. The internet was once seen as an instrument that allowed the average person access to near limitless information; however, the widespread availability of information has had the unintended consequence of the the breakdown of trust throughout society, as fringe views can seem mainstream.

■ **Why should the rise of mistrust and breakdown of truth concern us as Christians?**

As Christians, we hold to objective truth that is not rooted in what we want or desire. Truth is a fixed reality outside of us rooted in the God of the universe who made us and everything else we know. He also determines what is true. Part of what it means to love God and others is to speak truth in love, even when it is inconvenient.

■ Do you hear "misinformation" and "fake news" more often associated with people you agree with or those with opposing viewpoints?

How common would you say "fake news" and "misinformation" are today? Why do you think these terms have recently gained traction as common words in public life?

Many of the terms that are common today are used without clear definitions. *Misinformation* refers to a very broad category of false or misleading information that is often spread unintentionally, sometimes without awareness of the false claims. While on the other hand, *disinformation* refers to the same type of information spreading intentionally, often for a particular purpose. The influence of fake news, misinformation, propaganda, disinformation, and conspiracy theories grows each day. Christians must be loving and thoughtful about how and when we engage these issues, given how tense these conversations have become in recent years.

■ **Read these verses, noticing the connection between love and truth.**

Love is patient, love is kind. Love does not envy, is not boastful, is not arrogant, is not rude, is not self-seeking, is not irritable, and does not keep a record of wrongs. Love finds no joy in unrighteousness but rejoices in the truth.
1 CORINTHIANS 13:4-6

What are some ways Christians can seek to be loving in the ways we share and interact with news and information online? How might our online interactions violate this type of love?

Paul also says that "love is patient." How might cultivating patience lead us to be more loving and careful in an age of misinformation?

Social media platforms like Twitter™ and Facebook™ encourage immediate responses to news and current events, often before the facts are even revealed. Within moments of something happening, our feeds are filled with hot takes and commentary. In a matter of days, some of our friends and neighbors (and maybe even you and I) become lawyers, policy experts, critics, doctors, engineers, and more on social media. We often speak without understanding or knowledge on important matters. But Christian love is patient, humble, and rejoices in the truth.

■ **Why are we tempted to comment on something or post on a subject that we aren't familiar with?**

The call of the Christian in the digital age amidst the crumbling foundations of truth is to see through the appeal and novelty of our latest gadgets to the core of the issues we are facing. Technology is shaping us each day to rage on social media but stay silent when it matters, seek shallowness over sustained study, and to ultimately treat our fellow image bearers as simply profile pictures to be dismissed and disregarded instead of people created in God's image.

PRAYER

Father, You have made us and know what is best for us. Even in the midst of the breakdown of truth we all experience, we know that You are good and are the Author of truth. Help us to trust You and seek to reflect You and Your truth always. In Jesus's name, amen.

Personal Study 1
LEARN

TRUTH FROM THE SOURCE

As Christians seek to navigate the wild world of technology today, we must keep at the forefront of our minds that technology is discipling and forming us in particular ways. The question we must continually ask is what image we are being conformed to: Christ or the world?

One of the main ways that technology shapes us is how we perceive truth. It is far too common, even amongst Christians, to claim that something is true because it aligns with our desires or our political preferences. It's just as common to claim something is false or "fake news" if it isn't helpful to our cause or doesn't align with our plan for ourselves or society.

While the problems we're facing predate the rise of digital technology, social media and internet culture has certainly contributed to the widespread nature of misinformation, fake news, and conspiracy theories. But is there a distinctly Christian way to view these issues in light of what the Bible says about truth?

■ **What are a few things the Bible teaches about the nature of truth?**

For Christians, one of the clearest teachings in Scripture is on the nature of truth. We believe that the God of the universe created all things and sustains us by the power of His hand. He gave us the ability for us to comprehend His greatness and truth. Even if our sin and rebellion cause us to deny Him, the truth has still been clearly perceived (Romans 1:20). Jesus gave Christians a foundational understanding of truth in the Gospel of John:

> *Jesus told him, "I am the way, the truth, and the life.*
> *No one comes to the Father except through me."*
> **JOHN 14:6**

In our quest to find truth and meaning in this world, we don't have to look any further than the person of Jesus Christ, the Son of God. Truth is defined by God and is always consistent with His creation and the way He calls His people to live (Psalm 86:11; John 16:13; 1 Corinthians 14:33). He does not contradict Himself or lead us into falsehood. When we are seeking truth in the digital age, our first order of business should naturally be to ask: *What does Scripture say about this?*

Truth is essential to God's character. As people of God, we are to be committed to truth. We can often simplify this into thinking that pursuing truth only means believing the right things about God (theology). However, pursuing truth also includes our actions (ethics) including our commitment to tell and share the truth.

■ **What does it mean that Jesus is the way? The truth? The life?**

How do we distort these realties as we seek to determine our own truth apart from Christ's presence and revelation?

What do you think it means to be committed to truth-telling? How does this extend beyond our words?

If Jesus is truth, what are some ways you can grow in your knowledge of truth?

CHRISTIAN COMMITMENT TO TRUTH

This commitment to tell and share the truth is essential to Christian living. For one, we are called to be a Great Commission people, devoted to take and share the gospel amongst all nations (Matthew 28:18-20; Acts 1:8). And as we have already seen, the Great Commission is never at odds with the Great Commandment, to "love the Lord your God with all your heart, with all your soul, and with all your mind" and to "love your neighbor as yourself" (Matthew 22:37-39). In our obedience to these commands by Jesus, we are to make the truth known throughout the entire world.

In another way, our commitment to the truth may be best stated by negation: a commitment to not spread lies or false witness. The Ten Commandments forbid bearing false witness (or lying) about your neighbor (Exodus 20:16). According to Proverbs, "A false witness will not go unpunished, and one who utters lies perishes" (Proverbs 19:9). The language here is serious. No cause or action is important enough for us to spread misinformation or speak falsely toward others. But you might ask, *What about spreading half-truths or misleading information for the greater good?*

■ **Read Joshua 2 and summarize what happened.**

Notice what God shows us through this passage. Rahab lied, but she was concerned about God's mission and His desires. While Scripture never condones her half-truths, it does commend her faith (Hebrews 11:31 and James 2:25). Rahab had heard about the works of the Lord and was committed to serving Him. Her outward-focused love in protecting the spies serves as a model for us as the church today rather than a license to break God's commandments to share mistruth for likes or personal gain.

This should act as a warning to us in the digital age, especially with the rise of misinformation. What we share with others matters and it would be wise to make sure that what we are sharing or believing is actually true before we put our own integrity on the line by sharing things with others.

■ How does a commitment to truth-telling set Christians apart in digital spaces?

What would change about your willingness to share mistruths if you focused more on obeying God and honoring others rather than looking for exceptions to the "rules" and justification for lies?

How can you be more discerning when it comes to "fake news" and "misinformation" that you encounter online?

PUT ON THE NEW SELF

Discerning truth online is critical in the digital age. In a political climate that is becoming increasingly more partisan, truth sometimes takes a back seat to ideas and stories that help rally tribes around a social or political cause. The words of the apostle Paul in his letter to the Ephesians are instructive on how Christians need to posture themselves in relation to truth and to others. Paul writes,

> But that is not how you came to know Christ, assuming you heard about him and were taught by him, as the truth is in Jesus, to take off your former way of life, the old self that is corrupted by deceitful desires, to be renewed in the spirit of your minds, and to put on the new self, the one created according to God's likeness in righteousness and purity of the truth. Therefore, putting away lying, speak the truth, each one to his neighbor, because we are members of one another.
> **EPHESIANS 4:20-25**

■ **What does it look like to "put away the old self" when it comes to your social media sharing?**

If you're honest, do you treat the command to speak the truth as a command or a suggestion? Explain.

It's because of our salvation in Jesus Christ, who is the truth, that we can rid ourselves of the desire to do what is deceitful. Christ reminds us that we are committed to the truth because we are a new creation in him. We are to put away lying, selfish gain, and even the common idea today that we are able to bend the truth so long as we serve ourselves and our cause.

Without a commitment to Christ as the truth, it makes sense that some would seek to alter reality to fit their desires and will. Without the fixed nature of reality under the Lordship of Christ, it only makes sense that we would see ourselves as able to define and shape our own realities.

Throughout our society and our churches, we have seen countless friends, family members, and loved ones be deceived by fake news, misinformation, and conspiracy theories online, often out of a desire to be seen as the insider or as one who knows what's really going on and is on the right side of an issue. Today, truth is often defined by what is convenient or what helps our tribe put points on the board, rather than a fixed reality outside of us.

■ **Why should knowing that truth is not conditional or relative but fixed in God's character and His eternal purposes be comforting to us?**

■ **How does that help us continue to tell the truth when it is inconvenient or costly?**

Since Christians are people who believe in absolute truth, what impact does it have on our witness if we become known as people who share misinformation and conspiracy theories?

Whether it's out of ignorance, a failure to be careful, or even intentionally, many of us brush off sharing falsehoods online because it often seems as though no one is really harmed. Even though truth-telling is commanded in Scripture we think the failure to obey that command is somehow excusable. One of the most overlooked consequences of sharing misinformation is the damage it does to the public witness of the church. If Christians traffic in disinformation and conspiracy theories, how can we expect our neighbors to believe us when it comes to the truth of the gospel? Ultimately, the truth is what sets us free. Christians should be known as people committed to truth.

■ **How has this study challenged or reaffirmed your commitment to being truthful?**

Personal Study 2
INFLUENCE

Being committed to the truth and living consistently with that truth is one of the most important aspects of the Christian life. This is one of the main themes we see throughout Scripture but also one of the main purposes behind the Wisdom books, including Job, Ecclesiastes, Psalms, Proverbs, the Song of Solomon, James, and even some of Jesus's teachings in the Gospels. These texts are helpful for navigating many of the tensions we face today as they encourage God's people to order our lives and society in ways that honor God as well as point us to the ultimate end of enjoying Him.

Think about the circumstances in which the biblical wisdom literature itself was given to Israel. As the winds of cultural and social instability swirled around the people of God, He spoke to them a word of wisdom and peace that still guides us today as we engage a society that has lost its bearing in terms of what is real and what is fake. Isn't it encouraging to know that Scripture was not written in some ivory tower, divorced from real life?

The wisdom literature reminds us that God has spoken certain truths and that those truths are to be lived out in every aspect of our lives, personally, as a family, as a church, and as a community. No matter where you are, who you are with, or what you are doing, being committed to telling and sharing the truth should be second nature for the Christian as we attest to the realities of who God is and what He has done for us in Jesus Christ.

In our families, honesty is key as it allows for trust in the constant relationship of living together and taking care of each other. At work, transparency on the value of and means for accomplishing the work is needed to motivate and encourage those working towards it. In the church, not only are we seeking and sharing the truth through sound teaching and discipleship, but we are also being truthful with each other. In the words that we say, we look to build up and encourage one another rather than deceive those with whom we have fellowship. And as individuals who interact and engage with others in digital and nondigital spaces, we must always be aware of the ways we might be deceiving ourselves or unintentionally deceiving others with what we share online and the things we follow.

■ How have you sacrificed truth for convenience in your personal or family life? Where have you fallen short of this standard with your friends or spouse?

Does your standard for telling and witnessing to the truth change depending on what environment you are in (home, work, with your friends, online)? If so, why?

How do you talk about misinformation and fake news at work, with your family, or your neighbors?

What do you need to do to better address these competing narratives on truth that circulate in places you live, work, and spend your free time?

Personal Study 3
PRACTICE

In this fast-paced digital age, it is not uncommon for us to share information without actually reading it. For some of us that might seem ludicrous. How can you share something with other people, putting your own integrity and credibility on the line, without even having read what you are sharing? This is one of the reasons we have seen some social media companies over the last few years add some friction before we share something online like a message that reads, "Do you want to read the article before sharing it?" or, "This article has been flagged as potentially misleading or promoting falsified information."

Given the complexities of our cultural moment in regards to how many are seeking to redefine reality based on personal preference and desires, it is wise to slow down and ask the hard questions about our social media and technology habits, including how and why we share the things we do online and in person. There is wisdom in being patient with information and news today, as it can help prevent us from accidentally sharing fake news and misinformation.

■ **What kinds of articles and posts do you like and share? What do those communicate about what you value?**

How does what you follow or seek out online shape what your value?

Do you have friends whom you bounce ideas or posts off of before sharing them online? If so, have they stopped or cautioned you about posting something before? If not, who in your life could you ask to review things before you post or comment on social media and the internet?

One of the greatest ways to help overcome the temptation to spread information for self-interest is to cultivate a reciprocal relationship with a spouse, close friend, or group of friends to text or talk to about the things you may want to say or post online. This friction can help slow you down from making big mistakes in the heat of the moment and/or unintentionally spreading misinformation online.

■ **What are some practical ways you can care for those who are caught in the trap of fake news and misinformation?**

■ **What kind of personal habits can you seek to cultivate in order to develop a Christ-centered commitment to truth and honesty?**

If we are committed to truth-telling and sharing in a holistic manner, we will look to cultivate truthful, honest communities wherever we are. As Christians, in our personal lives, homes, work environments, and churches, we should champion truth because God desires His people to be truthful with each other. Let God dictate how we are to think about and engage with all different kinds of narratives that are claiming to be true, yet in contradiction with each other. And above all, let us continually seek to follow Jesus faithfully in this digital age.

Week 5
RELATIONSHIPS

» START

Use this section to get the conversation going.

Digital technologies, like the internet and social media, were built on two great promises: deeper connections with others and more access to information than we could ever imagine which would usher in a new era of freedom. Last week, we looked at how technology shapes our approach to and understanding of truth; this week, we'll be focusing on relationships. The early days of online platforms were full of promise and excitement about connecting the world and developing rich community with others, especially around shared causes, ideas, and common interests.

■ **How have you seen social media fulfill those promises—deeper connection and more access to information?**

In recent years, though, we have seen the flip side of these once utopian promises of connection and freedom. Many of the reasons you decided to participate in this study are connected to these broken promises. Despite lofty goals, increasingly people are recognizing the isolation that many of us feel despite all of the "connections" and "friendships" that are mediated through these online platforms and apps.

■ **Have you ever "met" a friend or coworker for the first time virtually? Describe that experience.**

You may now have more friends, followers, and connections because of these tools than you once did, but most people don't feel more connected, loved, and truly known. Study after study shows that many of us feel more isolated, lonely, and disconnected than ever before. But how can that be, given the vast communities and networks we are a part of online? Were all of the connections and community overhyped and overpromised or did something just go wrong? That's what we're going to explore this week.

» WATCH

Use this space to take notes during the video.

» DISCUSS

One of the biggest draws of the digital age is that we can keep in touch with more people now than ever before. The family that you once were only able to talk to a few times a year are now accessible through video calls, virtual photo albums, and social posts at any time. Those college friends that moved away to start their careers don't feel that far way since we can follow them online. Parents can check in on their kids, both young and old, to know what they are up to without even having to pick up the phone or feeling like they are bothering them with texts or phone calls.

■ **Who in your life have you kept up with through technology and social media?**

How has technology helped you stay more connected with people?

In what ways have these tools strengthened your relationships?

In some ways, our culture is the most connected time we have ever lived in as a society. But for all the good of these tools, most of us can easily feel the difference between the genuine connections we have in person with others and the ones we have only digitally. Despite the online connections we have access to, we all long to be truly present in community with one another.

Although it's possible to meaningfully connect through digital means, there is a clear level of longing, excitement, and joy when we get to hug each other for the first time in a long time or finally get to be together in person. There is just something about being with someone that we can't recreate digitally, and there is a depth and openess that we can't achieve online.

■ **Why do in-person connections and relationships feel more genuine or authentic to us as human beings?**

What types of things do you feel are lacking when you only connect with someone online or through social media?

We tend to think of connecting through technology as a new development, but human beings have connected through technology for thousands of years. When Paul wrote letters to churches, he expressed his longing to be with them in person, rather than to communicate through letters which was the communication technology of his day (2 Timothy 1:4). We may not be able to articulate exactly why we long for that type of physical connection, but we can all acknowledge that nothing truly satisfies those desires or takes the place of being fully present with others, both in body and in spirit.

We all long to be truly loved by others and to be truly known by them as well. As pastor Tim Keller once wrote, "To be loved but not known is comforting but superficial. To be known and not loved is our greatest fear. But to be fully known and truly loved is, well, a lot like being loved by God. It is what we need more than anything."[3]

■ **What can our relationships with other people teach us about our relationship with God and vice versa?**

Relationships were never designed to be transactional, nor performative where we always put our best foot forward in hopes that others won't see the worst. While there are obvious benefits to the types of connections we have today, we must work hard in order to guard against these things. But the lack of depth in our relationships is not limited only to the digital age, it has been a long-time problem in light of our broken relationship with God and others since the Fall in Genesis 3. But that doesn't mean that digital technologies made them any easier or authentic.

■ **Read Romans 12:1-2 together. What might it look like to not be conformed to this age in regard to relationships both digitally and in person?**

A downside to our digital existence is the temptation is to always be thinking about what others think about us or to longingly look at others, thinking that their life must be so much better than ours.

■ **Have you ever felt disconnected to others even though you are "connected" through digital means like social media? Share your experience with your group.**

Why do you constantly feel drawn to your device even if it routinely doesn't fulfill its promises to you?

Cultivating and deepening relationships with others is a key aspect of following Jesus in our digital age, as it take wisdom and thoughtfulness to use these tools well rather than let them use us. Through slowing down to ask some of these hard questions, setting wise boundaries and limits, and being aware of the effects technology can have on our relationships, we can hope to use these tools in light of biblical wisdom for the love of God and love of neighbor (Matthew 22:37-39).

PRAYER

Father, thank You for sending Your Son to us and for His sacrifice on the cross that we might have a relationship with You. Help us to use the tools You have given us wisely to love others well as we seek to build meaningful and deep relationships in our digital age. In Jesus's name, amen.

LEARN

How we relate to one another is one of the most defining aspects of being a Christian in the world today. In fact, how we see and relate to one another often reflects how we see and relate to God as well. If we want to cultivate authentic and godly relationships in the digital age then the best place to start is to look at how God relates to us, along with His instruction on how we are to relate to others.

One of the main passages we have been studying so far is Matthew 22:37-39. We are all called by God to love Him and to love our neighbor as ourselves. This type of love is directed outside of us and is meant to mark the Christian in a world of self-centered love and relationships. The apostle John expands on these words of Christ in another example of this other-directed love when he writes,

> I give you a new command: Love one another. Just as I have loved you, you are also to love one another. By this everyone will know that you are my disciples, if you love one another.
> **JOHN 13:34-35**

Jesus taught that our love for and relationships with other people are rooted in the way He loves us. God loves us despite our flaws or our perceived worth to others. He knows us intimately—even the aspects of our life that we don't want to share with others. We do not have any sense of privacy with God. He knows more about us than we even know about ourselves (Luke 12:7). His love informs how we love others and reveals our new identity in Christ as a member of His body (Romans 12:4-5).

This kind of love comes naturally when we're dealing with people we love; but for others, like a quarrelsome family member, a difficult work colleague, or even a social media troll, it is easier said than done. But true relationships are a two-sided affair and your love may not always be reciprocated. As Paul remind us, "If possible, as far as it depends on you, live at peace with everyone" (Romans 12:18). You are not responsible for how someone else receives you or your love, but that doesn't lessen God's standard to love your neighbor as yourself.

It can be tempting to treat the person on the other side of an online exchange as someone less deserving of your love. Without thinking we can treat people as merely a profile picture to dismiss rather than a person made in the image of God. In place of meaningful relationships we often see shallow, transactional, or even confrontational relationships, especially online.

But the body of Christ is called to a higher standard of love—no matter the medium—because our love for one another illustrates that we are true disciples of Jesus Christ, being conformed to His image and likeness rather than conformed to this world. This type of love will defy the world's expectations and set Christians apart.

■ **How have you experienced God's unconditional love for you in your life?**

How did you treat God before you became a Christian? Were you always kind or gracious? Did God pursue you anyways, despite your initial rejection of Him?

In what ways has God's love changed the way you think about and approach relationships?

What are some defining characteristics of your strongest friendships and relationships?

How has technology helped these relationships or damaged them?

Whether we want to acknowledge it or not, the way we interact with people online shows what we believe about how we should relate to one another. But if we take a quick look at our social media feeds, even among Christians, can we really say with confidence that we are known by our love on those mediums? In light of what Jesus tells about how we will be known as His disciples, this observation should trouble us all the more. What we say, do, and post on social media matters. God sees it all—including the things we only think about posting but never do. He sees our heart's intent in posting or engaging with others online. Our Christian responsibility to love others is a nonnegotiable. Our love for others must be front and center at all times, in all spaces, including digital ones. How else will other know that we are His disciples (John 13:34-35)?

■ **How would you describe the quality of conversation and relationships in digital spaces?**

How have your relationships with others been affected by the way digital spaces promote quick, often shallow responses and a desire to be right, rather than speaking the truth in love?

The reason why it may be easier to attack or be unkind to people online is the simple fact that we are not dealing with the fully embodied person, but only his or her ideas and words. Obviously, what we say reflects what we believe and desire, but when dealing with people online rather than face-to-face, it is easier to reduce them to the things we hear them say, or what we hear others say about them. When that happens we begin to see people as just the sum of their ideas rather than human beings just like us.

We are all guilty of doing this to someone at times. Many of the technologies we use today seem to encourage us to see other people as merely online accounts rather than human beings. In the same way, others are guilty of doing the same to you. Part of this is the reality of living in a digital age, but regardless of how technology is shaping and discipling us we must push back against these lies as Christians and demonstrate love for all people—even those with whom we disagree on important issues.

In fact, it seems that this lack of love is often most prevalent within our Christian circles. It is often easier for Christians to brush off how non-Christians treat us, but the way that our brothers and sisters in Christ treat us cuts a bit deeper and often leaves a deeper wound because of how close they are to us.

But Paul calls all of us to communicate with one another in a different way. One that sees people for what they are worth, what their true identity is, rather than simply as the product of their ideas or beliefs. In Ephesians 4, Paul writes,

> Therefore I, the prisoner in the Lord, urge you to walk worthy of the
> calling you have received, with all humility and gentleness, with
> patience, bearing with one another in love, making every effort
> to keep the unity of the Spirit through the bond of peace. There
> is one body and one Spirit—just as you were called to one hope
> at your calling—one Lord, one faith, one baptism, one God and
> Father of all, who is above all and through all and in all.
> **EPHESIANS 4:1-6**

■ **List all the instructions Paul gives in the passage on the previous page.**

Paul was instructing the community of believers, but his wisdom here should not be confined to corporate gathering. This instruction should be the prerogative of all Christians as they seek to cultivate relationships with believers and nonbelievers alike.

As Christians seek to cultivate authentic relationships in our digital age, we must seek to walk in a way that is worthy of Christ. Seeking unity over division. Carrying each other's burdens rather than piling on. Pursuing peace with one another, instead of stirring up quarrels. Speaking truth in love as we follow after Jesus and seek to love God as well as our neighbors.

Digital tools allow for more consistent communication with others but can also discourage us from cultivating deep, authentic relationships, especially with people who think and believe differently than us. The way social media allows us to build our online environments and follow specific kinds of groups or thinkers can be harmful because we are less likely to be challenged to think through what we believe and why we believe it. It also feeds the idea that we simply have nothing in common with those whom we disagree on important matters.

The church is made up of a diverse group of believers from every tribe, tongue, and nation because of God's call on all of us to pursue Great Commission work, to take the gospel to the nations. Cultivating deep relationships both with those whom we agree and disagree with is a key tenet of this Great Commission work.

■ **What qualities do you enjoy about those people with whom you have the deepest relationships?**

How has technology affected the way you think about those different from you? Does it encourage or discourage deep relationships with those who think differently than you do? Explain.

What types of things might you have in common with those whom you disagree with on major social and political issues?

How might technology help you cultivate deeper relationships with others, especially those you disagree with?

Personal Study 2
INFLUENCE

We have the privilege of interacting with different types of people across different areas of life. For many of us, the people we have relationships with, whether at home, work, or in public, are diverse in age, race, and beliefs. How we relate to people in different life situations depends on the relationship we have with them; for example, a father relates differently to his child than his boss at work. Or a coworker versus someone you met and only interact with online. Regardless of the medium, we're still called to love God and love our neighbor as ourselves. Our goal is to cultivate deep relationships with others that model the love we have received from God, but this requires vulnerability, intentionality, and respect. Note that this will vary based on the type of relationship you have with another person, but this doesn't mean that we can be unloving toward others even if that love looks different in different environments.

■ **How do your relationships with friends and family differ from your relationships with work colleagues or neighbors?**

Some of our relationships are primarily maintained through digital communication such as text messages, phone calls, and social media. But can this lead to the deep connection we want to have with those closest in our lives? One of the great promises of our digital age was that we would have deep connections with people around the world and even down the street given how easy it is to communicate and share common interests.

■ **How might technology actually be hindering your ability to build deep and lasting relationships with others?**

■ **In light of the other topics we have studied so far, what type of barriers might be present as you seek to engage others in deeper relationships both digitally and in person?**

There is a good chance that when you go out in public, get the family together, or check the break room at work during your lunch break, what you'll see is a lot of individuals who are all captivated by something other than the people in the room with them. Our devices often take over our attention completely as we are lost in a world of social media and connections that tell us the world is all about us. We all get lost on our phones, whether we are catching up on the news, seeing what our friends are up to, or even mindless scrolling on social media. While we are physically present with one another, mentally we are in a completely different place.

■ **What is it about social media and technology that turns us inward rather than focusing on others who are present with us?**

How can you intentionally push back against the temptation to get lost in the digital spaces in favor of in-person conversations?

How might technology tempt us to see other people as simply a means to an end? How can we seek to overcome those temptations and proclaim the value of every human being as made in the image of God?

Personal Study 3
PRACTICE

One of the major crossroads we often find ourselves at in this digital age is how to use technology with wisdom. As we have already covered in this study, technology is indeed a tool but one that is part of a larger culture and one that has profound effects on each of us—discipling us and shaping our view of the world in very particular, yet subtle ways. It can alter the nature of our relationships with others, and often tempts us to think of other people in terms of their value to us rather than to God our Creator.

It can be easy for us to think of all of the bad or all of the good ways it affects our relationships, but wisdom calls us to a higher place, one rooted in the love of God and love of neighbor. Seeing the complexities of how technology is discipling us and molding our interactions with others can open new doors for engaging technology and following Jesus in wisdom throughout our digital age.

■ **Take a moment to think about the people you interact with online. Write some of their names below. Include people you only know online. Next, write down the medium where you most often interact with them.**

Next, answer the following questions about them and think about how God views that person.

How is technology aiding your pursuit of this relationship, or how is it allowing you to neglect deeper connections through shallow connections?

When is the last time you prayed for these people?

How might you use technology as a crutch for keeping up with people?

How might you prioritize this relationship and seek to love this person better?

One of the more damaging effects of technology is that it can become a substitute for in-person relationships, where we think interacting online can make up for deepening relationships offline.

■ **What might it look like to prioritize relationships with those who you can see in person?**

We can thank God for the good gifts of technology and social media, even as we recognize the ways that these tools are shaping our perspective of the world and our interactions with others. Following Jesus in a digital age doesn't mean rejecting technology outright but understanding what it is and how it is shaping us. As we seek to cultivate and grow in our relationships with others, use these tools with wisdom and a higher purpose no matter how they may be marketed to us.

Week 6

WISDOM

» START

Use this section to get the conversation going.

■ **What kinds of notifications do you receive from your phone? How do you know when to acknowledge them and when to ignore them?**

We live in a day of information overload, which Alan Jacobs describes as "a sense that we are always receiving more sheer data than we know how to evaluate."[4] Our devices are full of countless messages, emails, to-do items, calendar updates, social media posts, likes, follows, shopping deals, shipping updates, parent chats to keep up with the shenanigans of our kids at school, notifications from our doorbell cameras, and even the score of last night's game.

■ **How does using devices limit your effectiveness in other areas of life (as a parent, friend, employee, etc.)?**

Have you noticed that we always keep our phones within arm's reach and grow uneasy if the service goes down even for a moment? Author and technology researcher Sherry Turkle even goes beyond the idea of "arm's reach" and describes our devices as arms themselves, or rather our "phantom limbs," since they never leave our side, and we often feel like we are missing part of us if we cannot access them.[5]

We are overwhelmed by the amount of information and the connectivity we have access to today. Throughout this study, we've talked about how technology is a tool, but one that is radically shaping how we see the world around us and is discipling us in subtle, yet distinct ways. We have seen how technology is altering how we perceive the nature of truth, our relationships with God and others, and even how we think about our role in society.

As we come to the end of this study, you may be asking yourself, *What are we supposed to do about it all?* This week we are going to be talking about using technology with wisdom.

» WATCH

Use this space to take notes during the video.

» DISCUSS

One of the threads that has run throughout this study is the concept of wisdom. In a world of quick fixes, technological gadgets, and checklists, we naturally long for a step-by-step guide for shoring up our digital habits or for overcoming our addictions to technology. We want a quick fix, but we need wisdom.

■ **When we talk about the idea of wisdom, what comes to your mind?**

Who are some people that model wisdom in your life? What is it about them that makes you consider them wise?

While we have seen that technology constantly pushes us toward more, better, faster, God's Word reveals to us a different path through the digital age that is grounded in biblical wisdom and moral responsibility. Once we see the immense power of technology, we can despair, or we can proceed with wisdom as the key to navigating the digital age—because biblical wisdom is how God calls us to live no matter what we face, whether that be a den of lions in Daniel's day or digitally connected society in our own. Wisdom is a key to understanding how God calls His people to act in a world saturated by technology.

■ **Read Proverbs 2:1-6. What does the author (Solomon) compare wisdom to? Where does wisdom come from? How should we similarly think about wisdom in our digital age?**

For the Christian, the Bible has a wealth of pages devoted to wisdom, in both the Old and the New Testament. Living with wisdom in light of the truth we know and believe is a consistent theme throughout Scripture. It is important for Christians to continually seek out the answer to the question, *What does it mean to be wise according to the Bible?*

■ **How has the Bible helped you grow in wisdom?**

Brett McCracken wrote a book on wisdom called *The Wisdom Pyramid* and in it he draws from the traditional food pyramid substituting different mediums from which we acquire truth and knowledge. He argues that wisdom should be drawn from the Bible first before going through the next five areas in order:

- Church/Tradition
- Nature and Beauty
- Books
- Internet
- Social Media

■ **Why are internet and social media at the top part of the pyramid (in other words, to play the smallest role and to be used the least)?**

How has social media made you think/feel about news and information in the past year? Do you feel better informed and wiser or do you feel more overwhelmed and exhausted?

Do you feel like social media is a good place to get news and information? What advantages could there be but also what are some of the possible dangers or drawbacks?

Here are a few principles to pursuing wisdom in our digital age.

First, we all need to slow down and take time to think biblically about all of life. Wisdom is a slow process and is gained over a lifetime, not overnight.

Second, wisdom is cultivated not in isolated individualistic thinking, but in a community/group (like this one). Talking to and learning from others, even those whom you disagree with, is a great benefit to Christians.

Finally, wisdom is seen in the deep and interdependent relationship of belief and action, or theology and ethics. What we believe shapes what we do and what we do reveals what we truly believe.

Wisdom is truth applied, and for the Christian wisdom looks like people living and looking more like Christ who is the true Wisdom Himself, as He always submitted to and obeyed the truth of God's Word (1 Corinthians 1:24).

■ **In what ways might your actions and your beliefs not be aligned? What do you claim to believe but fail to live out in your life?**

How are our technologies forming us in ways contrary to wisdom?

PRAYER

Lord, all truth is Your truth. Help us to come to a greater understanding of who You are and what You are doing in our lives. Help us better understand who we are and how You are calling us to live in this world. May we seek wisdom in all things, especially in navigating the tough questions about technology and social media in this digital age. Let us not forget what You have called us to do and who You have called us to be. Help us use the tools You have blessed us with for Your glory. In Jesus's name, amen.

Personal Study 1
LEARN

Pursuing wisdom today seems like a tall order. As we have discussed, we are inundated with countless bits of information. Our timelines and feeds are full of things we need to know and likely a ton of things we don't really care to know about. Years before the internet and social media, Neil Postman wrote about information overload as the "now . . . this" problem describing how most modern TV news anchors would give you about forty-five seconds to think about something before exclaiming "and now . . . this."[6] Our attention would be turned to a catastrophic international event and forty-five seconds later we would be introduced to a human-interest piece, followed by a few commercials, and then yet again another set of forty-five-second news stories. But in our digital age, forty-five seconds is a luxury as we may spend less than a few seconds reading a headline before moving on to the next tweet, post, or video.

We are swimming in information with what feels like little to no hope to navigate it wisely.

Outside of the amount of information we are overwhelmed by each day, it may be hard for us to identify what wisdom looks like. Technology has radically altered how we see each other, and how we all process the times in which we live. When some of us think about wisdom, we may even think of fictional characters like Gandalf or Yoda since we have very few examples of wise men and women in our lives. I think part of our problem in identifying the wise people in our lives is that we are often tempted to only see the flashy, loud, and publicly influential people in society today. Combine that with how wisdom is cultivated over a lifetime and that many of the wisest among us don't feel the need to shout it from the rooftops. Thus, we quickly see why wisdom might seem so rare.

So, what is wisdom and how do we pursue it? In the Bible, the clearest window into the nature of wisdom is found in the section of the Bible referred to as wisdom literature.

The wisdom literature includes the books of Ecclesiastes, Psalms, Proverbs, Job, the Song of Solomon, James, and even some of Jesus's teachings seen in the

Gospels. These texts are rich with insight and helpful for navigating many of the tensions we face today, as they encourage God's people to order our lives and society in ways that honor God as well as point us to the ultimate end of enjoying Him forever. Biblical wisdom is how God calls us to live no matter what we face.

Consider Proverbs 2:1-10:

> *My son, if you accept my words and store up my commands within you, listening closely to wisdom and directing your heart to understanding; furthermore, if you call out to insight and lift your voice to understanding, if you seek it like silver and search for it like hidden treasure, then you will understand the fear of the LORD and discover the knowledge of God. For the LORD gives wisdom; from his mouth comes knowledge and understanding. He stores up success for the upright; He is a shield for those who live with integrity so that he may guard the paths of justice and protect the way of his faithful followers. Then you will understand righteousness, justice, and integrity—every good path. For wisdom will enter your heart, and knowledge will delight you.*
> **PROVERBS 2:1-10**

Wisdom in the Bible—especially in the book of Proverbs—is not only aimed at revealing a set of theological truths that we need to believe, but also at cultivating a life of godliness in light of a healthy reverence of God.

In short, wisdom isn't just believing the right truths, it's how to live in light of those truths. A wise person submits all of life, including technology habits, to the Lord, seeking to use technology with integrity, righteousness, and justice. This is not always the easy thing to do, since technology is constantly pushing toward a vision of life that is often contrary to the Word of God (Romans 12:2). It has become so commonplace in our digital age that we never slow down and ask the hard questions about technology outside of what convenience it may bring.

For the Christian, Proverbs calls us to do something completely different—to understand these tools and to use them for good and right purposes.

■ **What are some of the traits or characteristics that a wise person will model from Proverbs 2:1-10?**

How has God called His people to live in light of biblical wisdom?

Consider what technologies you use every day. How have you been using them wisely (with justice, righteousness, and integrity)?

Proverbs 9:9-10 says,

Instruct the wise, and he will be wiser still; teach the righteous, and he will learn more. The fear of the LORD is the beginning of wisdom, and the knowledge of the Holy One is understanding.
PROVERBS 9:9-10

Think about how verse 10 calls us to "fear the Lord" which is the "beginning of wisdom." Fearing God doesn't mean that we are afraid of or nervous around Him, but that we are to have a healthy reverence for Him based on who He is as God and our Creator. Wisdom, even for the digital age, must begin with recognizing who God is and how He calls us to live. He not only created us in His image but has spoken to us through His Word about what we are to do in light of those truths (Matthew 22:37-39).

■ **Why is it important to pursue and cultivate biblical wisdom and why is that so important in the Christian life as we engage the toughest questions of our day?**

How does pursing wisdom help us to love God and love our neighbors (Matthew 22:37-39)?

Does your use of technology model the fruit of the Spirit (Galatians 5:22-23)? Remember that we are called to model all of those traits, not just the ones that come easier to us.

While we cannot truly escape the formative power of technology, we also are not required to use any particular tool. If you are convicted about how you use a certain app, tools, or technology, pray and ask the Holy Spirit to reveal to you what it might look like to cultivate wisdom in that area. Maybe you need to put it down for a while, walk away entirely, or build some relationships with others that can keep you accountable. We have seen that the wisdom literature poses important challenges for Christians as we seek to live faithfully for the Lord in our digital world.

■ **Read Ecclesiastes 9:17-18.**

The calm words of the wise are heeded more than the shouts of a ruler over fools. Wisdom is better than weapons of war, but one sinner can destroy much good.
ECCLESIASTES 9:17-18

■ **How can this wisdom help you navigate technology, where your witness is on display and accessible to nearly everyone?**

In these two verses alone, there are three important principles for us to remember. First, calm words are still better than loud words. In a world today where the loudest voices often have the largest followings, it is important to remember that it is better to speak calmly and gently in the public square despite the shouting happening all around. Second, being wise is a greater advantage than having great weapons or opportunities to be recognized and heard by others. Third and finally, be aware of sin and how technology can expand our moral horizons, allowing us to do things that we never thought possible and to reach thousands instantaneously. In the past, certain vices may have been limited in scope, but due to the widespread nature of technology we can now reach more people than ever before and our sin can be on full display for the world to see. On digital platforms that often promote and leverage anger, outrage, and even sometimes wickedness, remember that above all Christians are to model for the world (and our followers) what it looks like to have a steadfast hope and peace even in the midst of cultural confusion and chaos.

■ **How do you model biblical wisdom and the fruit of the Spirit online today? Do you act differently on different platforms? Why?**

Do your conversations and interactions with others online look more like Christ or the way the world acts? Explain.

■ **How might you be employing the ways of the world as you interact or connect with other people online?**

Are you slow to speak, slow to anger, and quick to listen online or are you tempted to do the opposite (James 1:19)?

How can you model biblical wisdom on social media, especially with voices that you disagree with?

Based on all you've studied, what is one concrete step you have taken or will take to exercise wisdom in digital spaces?

Ask a friend what your presence on social media communicates to others. Tell them to be honest with you and that you want to grow in your awareness and wisdom online. Compare your answers to what they say.

Personal Study 2
INFLUENCE

Wisdom must be pursued in every area of our lives. That means that we must seek God's wisdom in our families, at school, in our jobs, at church, and anywhere else that God places us. We've already touched on what wisdom with technology looks like for the individual, including the responsibility to teach and instruct others in the ways of God as well as to model the fruits of the Spirit (Galatians 5:22-23).

But as we have already seen, God does not just call you as an individual to pursue holiness and wisdom. He calls His people to seek the good of others and the good of our communities. Remember Matthew 22:37-39 and how the entire law is summarized in the Great Commandment of loving God and loving others? Note that this love is pointed outward, outside of ourselves, even though the command is directly to us. We are each given the command as believers in Christ to love others, rather than to simply seek to love ourselves. In a culture that is fixated on living your truth, shirking personal responsibility for others, and even seeking to craft our personal identities online, God reminds His people that we shouldn't be focused on ourselves but on loving others as ourselves. We each have a personal responsibility to care for and seek the good of others, to model Christ's love and wisdom for others to see and experience as well.

Now, let's consider the different role and responsibility that God has given us. For example, as a spouse or roommate, it's so easy for us to get lost in our devices from time to time isn't it? We can fail to pay attention or focus on the person right in front of us as we claim we are just glancing at our phones for a minute. But with the way that technology envelopes us and inevitably shapes us as people, we can quickly shift from loving others as ourselves to simply loving ourselves. Seeking wisdom in this context may mean setting patterns and habits up in your life and marriage where you prioritize certain times to be with other people without phones or devices. This isn't about being legalistic but recognizing your own limits, temptations, and technology patterns.

We are to seek wisdom in our parenting as well. There are a number of technologies like a smartphone or tablet that you may feel it is important to withhold from your children for a time or until a certain age. At the same time, you may allow your kids to have their own devices, play video games, or watch TV. These decisions must be made in light of wisdom and the maturity of your child. Wisdom doesn't give you a checklist or a long list of tips/tricks in navigating these questions with your children. There just simply isn't a rule book for parenting, especially with technology.

Wisdom reminds us that we need to think deeply about technology, not only what it is but how it is shaping how we view the world. Now, take these examples and consider the different spheres you find yourself in. Consider what we read earlier in Proverbs 2:1-10, and remember one of the main differences between the wise person and the fool: virtue.

Virtue is the fruit of applying biblical wisdom into your life and becoming the type of person that God has called you to be. Cultivating wisdom and virtue is less about a set of rules and more about the type of person you are becoming. As we have discussed so far, technology is forming and discipling you in subtle, yet distinct ways. The question isn't are you being discipled, but by whom and to what end or purpose.

■ **What areas have you identified where you need to cultivate wisdom in your technology habits?**

How might your technology habits be altering your relationships with others in your family, workplace, or church?

What are some of the toughest questions regarding technology you have when you think about where God has placed you in this season?

Recognizing the way that technology is discipling us is the first step in pursuing wisdom in our digital age. It's far too easy for us to sit back and let these tools shape us toward the ways of this world (Romans 12:2) but wisdom reminds us that God is the one who is to form and shape us into the type of people whom He has called us to be in Christ. Wisdom pushes back against the ease, convenience, and luxury that technology promises. One way of cultivating wisdom in this arena is to think about some tangible ways to slow down and think deeply about these gifts you have been given.

■ **What does it mean to pursue virtue as you utilize these technological gifts that the Lord has given us? What should be your aim when using these tools?**

What are some possible next steps for addressing these tough questions you listed above?

Personal Study 3
PRACTICE

Even if this is your first time addressing your relationship with technology or how you use these tools in the workplace and home, trying to form new habits or change old ones can be a difficult task. Part of this difficulty spawns from how connected and dependent on technology we have become. Technology is not simply a tool that we use but is something that is in many ways using us, as it forms us into particular types of people often at odds with our faith, as we have discussed throughout this study.

It is important to understand that as difficult as it may be given the power and pull of technology in our lives, pursuing and cultivating wisdom is always part of God's plan for His people. If you become fainthearted on your journey of cultivating wisdom in the digital age, remember Proverbs 1:33 which says, "But whoever listens to me will live securely and be undisturbed by the dread of danger." God is not calling us to live some rigid form of obedience that is at odds with our ultimate good. He is calling us to live securely with Him knowing that He calls us to a greater purpose in life than the individualistic pursuit of freedom that is so common today. Wisdom reminds us of our dependence upon him and of his design for our entire lives, including our technology habits.

We have nothing to fear, dread, or ultimately lose when we seek after the Lord because he knows more about us and what we need than even we do (Matthew 6:25-34). Whatever bad habits need to be dropped, both personally or publicly, and whatever good habits need to be formed, remember that God holds you securely in this fast-paced, digital world we are living in. Remember Paul's words in Ephesians 4:20-24:

> But that is not how you came to know Christ, assuming you heard about him and were taught by him, as the truth is in Jesus, to take off your former way of life, the old self that is corrupted by deceitful desires, to be renewed in the spirit of your minds, and to put on the new self, the one created according to God's likeness in righteousness and purity of the truth.
> **EPHESIANS 4:20-24**

■ What are some of the former ways of thinking about technology and social media that you may need to "take off"?

What has God revealed to you in this study about your deceitful desires to seek your own good and fulfillment instead of to follow after Jesus with wisdom in our digital age?

Think back to our study of the fruit of the Spirit in Galatians 5:22-23: love, joy, peace, patience, kindness, goodness, faithfulness, gentleness, and self-control.

■ Consider each fruit and write down an action step for how you might cultivate each one in your use of technology this week.

What are some practices that we can cultivate in order to help us become wise people in our digital age?

FOLLOWING JESUS IN A DIGITAL AGE

Leader Guide

TIPS FOR LEADING A SMALL GROUP

PRAYERFULLY PREPARE

Prepare for each group session with prayer. Ask the Holy Spirit to work through you and the group discussion as you point to Jesus each week through God's Word.

REVIEW the personal study and the group sessions ahead of time.
PRAY for each person in the group.

MINIMIZE DISTRACTIONS

Do everything in your ability to help people focus on what's most important: connecting with God, with the Bible, and with one another. Try to put away technology and focus on your group.

CREATE A COMFORTABLE ENVIRONMENT. If group members are uncomfortable, they'll be distracted and therefore not engaged in the group experience.
TAKE INTO CONSIDERATION seating, temperature, lighting, refreshments, surrounding noise, and general cleanliness.

At best, thoughtfulness and hospitality show guests and group members they're welcome and valued in whatever environment you choose to gather. At worst, people may never notice your effort, but they're also not distracted.

INCLUDE OTHERS

Your goal is to foster a community in which people are welcome just as they are but encouraged to grow spiritually. Always be aware of opportunities to include and invite.
INCLUDE anyone who visits the group.
INVITE new people to join your group.

ENCOURAGE DISCUSSION

A good small group experience has the following characteristics.

EVERYONE PARTICIPATES. Encourage everyone to ask questions, share responses, or read aloud.

NO ONE DOMINATES—NOT EVEN THE LEADER. Be sure your time speaking as a leader takes up less than half your time together as a group. Politely guide the discussion if anyone dominates.

NOBODY IS RUSHED THROUGH QUESTIONS. Don't feel that a moment of silence is a bad thing. People often need time to think about their responses to questions they've just heard or to gain courage to share what God is teaching them.

INPUT IS AFFIRMED AND FOLLOWED UP. Make sure you point out something true or helpful in a response. Don't just move on. Build community with follow-up questions, asking how other people have experienced similar things or how a truth has shaped their understanding of God and the Scripture you're studying. People are less likely to speak up if they fear that you don't actually want to hear their answers or that you're looking for only a certain answer.

GOD AND HIS WORD ARE CENTRAL. Opinions and experiences can be helpful, but God has given us the truth. Trust Scripture to be the authority and God's Spirit to work in people's lives. You can't change anyone, but God can. Continually point people to the Word and to active steps of faith.

KEEP CONNECTING

THINK OF WAYS TO CONNECT with group members during the week. Participation during the group session always improves when members spend time connecting with one another outside the group sessions. The more people are comfortable with and involved in one another's lives, the more they'll look forward to being together. When people move beyond being friendly to truly being friends who form a community, they come to each session eager to engage instead of merely attending.

ENCOURAGE group members with thoughts, commitments, or questions from the session by connecting through emails, texts, and social media.

BUILD DEEPER FRIENDSHIPS by planning or spontaneously inviting group members to join you outside your regularly scheduled group time for meals; fun activities; and projects around your home, church, or community.

He said to him, "Love the Lord your God with all your heart, with all your soul, and with all your mind. This is the greatest and most important command. The second is like it: Love your neighbor as yourself."

MATTHEW 22:37-39

Session 1
TECHNOLOGY AND THE BIBLE

KEY PASSAGES

Deuteronomy 6:4-7

Ecclesiastes 2:14

Proverbs 9

Psalm 111

Matthew 22:37-39

BEFORE THE SESSION

- Review the group content as well as the video teaching session.
- Review the questions in the Start and Discuss sections and adjust as needed.
- Decide whether you're going to watch the video teaching sessions together or if you want group members to watch them prior to the group meeting. Each book includes codes to access the video teaching. Each video is around fifteen minutes long.
- Pray for all group members by name.

CONSIDER AS YOU LEAD

- Define technology—a tool that shapes and forms us in a particular way. Note that this goes beyond smartphones, computers, and the many things we consider "technology" today. Two of the most life-altering technologies in human history were the book and the printing press.

- This will likely be the first time that participants have taken the time to think deeply about the nature and role of technology in their lives. It might even be the first time you have done the same. Take it slow and push in on these questions and resources. Technology is one of the main disciplers of people and is something that's often hard for people to evaluate with clarity.
- The Bible speaks to all of life and God reveals to us a distinct way of living (an ethic) that informs how we are to respond to God's truth. But in order to do this, we must seek to slow down in a culture that is hooked on making things easier and more efficient to see how God is calling us to live in our digital age. In reality, the technology we use isn't really causing us to ask new questions of how to live per se, but to ask age-old questions in light of new opportunities and challenges.
- Watch the video teaching before hand and determine what you want to highlight from Jason's interviews. What do you want to point out to the group? What was most helpful? Consider asking the group what resonated with them in the interviews.

AS YOU CLOSE

- Explain the remaining sections of each session—Learn, Influence, Practice. Encourage them to complete the personal studies before the sessions. This will give them the best opportunity to truly interact with the material.
- Close in prayer.

AFTER THE SESSION

- Consider meeting in groups of two or three to discuss and review the personal studies.
- Send out some of the recommended resources for deeper study.
- Challenge the group to find additional passages where the Bible speaks to technology and meditate upon them.
- Send a midweek follow-up to connect and encourage.

Session 2
DISCIPLESHIP

KEY PASSAGES

Matthew 28:19-20
Galatians 5:22-25

Luke 14:25-27,33
2 Peter 1:3-8

BEFORE THE SESSION

- Review the group content as well as the video teaching session.
- Review the questions in the Start and Discuss sections and adjust as needed.
- Email the group and remind them of the meeting and any other house-keeping details.
- Pray for all group members by name.

CONSIDER AS YOU LEAD

- At the beginning of the group, challenge those present to see how often they are tempted to check phones and devices during the meeting. This isn't to shame them, but to help them gain an awareness of how connected and discipled we are by devices.
- Many in your group might feel that technology is disconnected from discipleship. This is why good discipleship beings with the end in mind. What kind of person do I want myself and the people in my group to become? What is the end goal for us? It should be to love God and love people (Matthew 22:37-39). How we use technology can take us closer or further away from that goal.
- Many people do not realize just how much their use of technology is shaping their life. Some may be actively engaged in tearing others down online or posting/sharing misinformation or even conspiracy theories. They may resist some of these ideas. Continue to press forward.

- This study is not a silver bullet that solves every challenge of the digital age, but it does seek to give a broader understanding of what is actually happening, every single day.
- When our eyes are opened to the issues at play in our digital age, we'll have much greater odds at countering the negative effects of technology as we pursue Christ in light of the Great Commandment.
- Watch the video teaching beforehand and determine what you want to highlight from Jason's interviews. What do you want to point out to the group? What was most helpful? Consider asking the group what resonated with them in the interviews.

AS YOU CLOSE

- Encourage the group to complete all three personal studies prior to the next meeting. Ask someone to share something they found particularity helpful in last week's personal study.
- Ask the group to spend the week considering how their devices and online accounts are discipling them. Challenge them to take a break even if it's just for a day or for an hour.
- Close in prayer.

AFTER THE SESSION

- Consider meeting in groups of two or three to discuss and review the personal studies.
- Send out some of the recommended resources for deeper study.
- Challenge the group to ask who they're discipling and who is discipling them. What impact does technology have on these relationships?
- Send a midweek follow-up to connect, encourage, and answer any lingering questions from the group session.

Session 3
IDENTITY

KEY PASSAGES

Proverbs 8:13

Matthew 5:43-44

Mark 8:34-38

Romans 12:2

Galatians 5:13-15

Colossians 4:2-6

BEFORE THE SESSION

- Review the group content as well as the video teaching session.
- Review the questions in the Start and Discuss sections and adjust as needed.
- Email the group and remind them of the meeting and any other house-keeping details.
- Pray for all group members by name.

CONSIDER AS YOU LEAD

- People might not realize all the ways they've pursued identity in lesser things rather than in who they are in Christ. It is all too common that people find their identity in others or seek to define it online. We are all guilty of it, and this identity crisis is on full display across our culture, especially on social media today.
- Lead the group to consider what picture someone would get of them based off who they followed and what they liked online.
- Having strong beliefs and convictions is good, but when defending those convictions become our sole identity, we've taken it too far.

- The beliefs we hold are important, as they help define who we are as people. Likewise, beliefs and actions both flow from who we are and what we believe. But every person you meet is far more complex than that and his or her value and worth is not rooted simply in what he or she believes but in whose image he or she has been created. Our ideas are not the sum total of our value and worth.
- Watch the video teaching beforehand and determine what you want to highlight from Jason's interviews. What do you want to point out to the group? What was most helpful? Consider asking the group what resonated with them in the interviews.

AS YOU CLOSE

- Encourage the group to complete all three personal studies prior to the next meeting.
- Ask the group to spend the week considering where they're finding their primary and secondary identity. Challenge them to adjust their gaze from temporal things to eternal things.
- Close in prayer.

AFTER THE SESSION

- Consider meeting in groups of two or three to discuss and review the personal studies.
- Send out some of the recommended resources for deeper study.
- Challenge the group to read through key passages from this week and consider where they're placing their identity.
- Send a midweek follow-up to connect, encourage, and answer any lingering questions from the group session.

Session 4
TRUTH

KEY PASSAGES

Psalm 86:11

Proverbs 19:9

John 14:6

John 16:13

1 Corinthians 14:33

Ephesians 4:20-25

1 Timothy 5:17

BEFORE THE SESSION

- Review the group content as well as the video teaching session.
- Review the questions in the Start and Discuss sections and adjust as needed.
- Email the group and remind them of the meeting and housekeeping details.
- Pray for all group members by name.

CONSIDER AS YOU LEAD

- Fake news, misinformation, and disinformation aren't just things that happen to other people. It happens to all of us. Consider sharing a story from your own life.
- Navigating a post-truth world can feel like an impossible task even for the most seasoned leaders. Every day your group is confronted with misinformation, conspiracy theories, and fake news and has the opportunity to spread these lies and half-truths for the world to see.
- If we don't come to these platforms and our use of technology with discernment and wisdom, we will be tossed by the waves of propaganda that often fills so many of our news sources today.
- Technology, while making truth more accessible, has also muddied the waters as to what is true in a given story or event, as it disciples us to believe that truth is in the eye of the beholder rather than something fixed and outside of us.

- Consider what the world sees when we post. What does you group see when you post? Likes, posts, shares, and retweets aren't as benign as we might assume. We should seek to represent Jesus in all that we say and do.
- We need to think deeply about our technology habits, not just for our own sake, but also for those around us who may consciously or unconsciously be looking to us for how to follow Jesus with wisdom in our digital age.
- Watch the video teaching beforehand and determine what you want to highlight from Jason's interviews. What do you want to point out to the group? What was most helpful? Consider asking the group what resonated with them in the interviews.

AS YOU CLOSE

- Encourage the group to complete all three personal studies.
- Reiterate that most of the time, the tweet or social post about a controversial topic isn't worth it. The sarcastic remark is unhelpful, and the offhand remark is unneeded. Remember that God calls us to a higher purpose.
- Ask the group to think twice before posting all week. Challenge them to ask themselves: Is this helpful? Is this Christlike? Is this true? Most social media has some kind of drafts feature, encourage them to use it and not be tempted to respond immediately and see how that changes their online presence.
- Encourage your group to text a friend before posting online this week.

AFTER THE SESSION

- Consider meeting in groups of two or three to discuss and review the personal studies.
- Send out some of the recommended resources for deeper study.
- Challenge the group to search the Scriptures for what they say about truth and to meditate on those passages.
- Send a midweek follow-up to connect, encourage, and answer any lingering questions from the group session.

Session 5
RELATIONSHIPS

KEY PASSAGES

John 13:34-35

Luke 12:7

Romans 12:4-5

Ephesians 4:1-6

BEFORE THE SESSION

- Review the group content as well as the video teaching session.
- Review the questions in the Start and Discuss sections and adjust as needed.
- Email the group and remind them of the meeting and any other house-keeping details.
- Pray for all group members by name.
- Think about what study you'll be doing next if your group will continue to meet beyond this study.

CONSIDER AS YOU LEAD

- Relationships can be a challenging area for all of us in a digital age. We feel like we are more connected than ever but often are more isolated and lonely.
- You will want to draw out how different relationships are online vs. offline with your group. What is missing from our relationships that are primarily mediated through digital means?
- It is far too easy for all of us to perform online in order to garner praise, influence, or followers. We routinely share and post things in order to gain more likes and shares, even if we don't consider ourselves to be influencers or in it for the praise of others.

- Encourage your group to start a text thread with other group members or close friends to share things they may normally post online. This can help deepen close relationships and build stronger friendships than simply tweeting or sharing things online for a larger group.
- Talk about which relationships are strongest in your life and what role social media plays in those relationships.
- Watch the video teaching beforehand and determine what you want to highlight from Jason's interviews. What do you want to point out to the group? What was most helpful? Consider asking the group what resonated with them in the interviews.

AS YOU CLOSE

- Encourage the group to complete all three personal studies prior to the next meeting.
- Ask the group to consider one relationship they're thankful for. Encourage them to reach out and encourage that person. Next ask them to think of one relationships where they've drifted apart or the friendship is strained. Encourage them to reach out and rekindle that friendship.
- Close in prayer.

AFTER THE SESSION

- Consider meeting in groups of two or three to discuss and review the personal studies.
- Send out some of the recommended resources for group members who want deeper study.
- During the week, challenge the group to evaluate their relationships and which ones need more time and attention.
- Send a midweek follow-up to connect, encourage, and answer any lingering questions from the group session.
- Let the group know what you plan to do after the end of this study.

Session 6
WISDOM

KEY PASSAGES

Proverbs 1:33

Proverbs 2:1-10

Ecclesiastes 9:17-18

Matthew 6:25-34

Ephesians 4:20-24

James 1:19

BEFORE THE SESSION

- Review the group content as well as the video teaching session.
- Review the questions in the Start and Discuss sections and adjust as needed.
- Email the group and remind them of the meeting and any other house-keeping details.
- Pray for all group members by name.
- Let the group know what you'll be doing next.

CONSIDER AS YOU LEAD

- Wisdom involves pursuing godly virtue and living with godly skill.
- In our digital age, it is far too easy to think that wisdom can be gained overnight or just by getting more information. But wisdom is a slow process and is gained over a lifetime. Submitting our entire lives to God and being formed more by His Word than our tools requires time and sacrifice.
- After all, we aren't called to pursue wisdom or to navigate this world alone. Not only were we created for community, but we are also members of the body of Christ if we are believers (Genesis 2:18; 1 Corinthians 12:12-31).
- You'll want to identify where you're seeking wisdom and consider the places group members might be seeking wisdom.

- Watch the video teaching beforehand and determine what you want to highlight from Jason's interviews. What do you want to point out to the group? What was most helpful? Consider asking the group what resonated with them in the interviews.

AS YOU CLOSE

- Encourage the group to complete all three personal studies prior to the next meeting.
- Ask the group to consider sources of wisdom. Where do they find wisdom? Is that source reliable? Where could they cultivate more godly wisdom?
- Thank the group for their time, attention, and discussion in this study.
- Close in prayer.

AFTER THE SESSION

- Consider meeting in groups of two or three to discuss and review the personal studies.
- Send out some of the recommended resources for group members who want deeper study.
- During the week, thank the group again for studying with you.
- Send a midweek follow-up to connect, encourage, and answer any lingering questions from the group session.
- Let the group know what you plan to do after the end of this study.

» RECOMMENDED RESOURCES

SESSION 1

- Jason Thacker, "Why doomsurfing won't satisfy our longing for peace," jasonthacker. com/2020/04/15/why-doomsurfing-wont-satisfy-our-longing-for-peace-2/.
- Jason Thacker, "How social media can impede our witness: The disconnect of the digital life," jasonthacker.com/2021/06/16/ how-social-media-can-impede-our-witness-the-disconnect-of-the-digital-life/.
- Podcast episode: "A conversation with Tony Reinke on a biblical theology of technology for the Christian life," jasonthacker.com/podcast/a-conversation-with-tony-reinke-on-a-biblical-theology-of-technology-for-the-christian-life/.

SESSION 2

- Jason Thacker, "Is Facebook discipling your church members?" erlc.com/ resource-library/articles/is-facebook-discipling-your-church-members/.
- Jason Thacker, "How social media can impede our witness: The disconnect of the digital life," jasonthacker.com/2021/06/16/ how-social-media-can-impede-our-witness-the-disconnect-of-the-digital-life/.
- Luke Holmes, "4 Ways Social Media Can Be Leveraged for Discipleship," research. lifeway.com/2020/10/13/4-ways-social-media-can-be-leveraged-for-discipleship/.
- Podcast episode: "A conversation with Dr. Felicia Wu Song on personhood, presence, and place in the digital age," jasonthacker.com/podcast/a-conversation-with-dr-felicia-wu-song-on-personhood-presence-and-place-in-the-digital-age/.

SESSION 3

- Jason Thacker, "How social media can impede our witness," erlc.com/resource-library/ articles/how-social-media-can-impede-our-witness/.
- Podcast Episode: Jason Thacker, "A conversation with Dr. Alan Noble on the false promises of contemporary life," jasonthacker.com/podcast/a-conversation-with-dr-alan-noble-on-the-false-promises-of-contemporary-life/.
- Jason Thacker, "How false notions of moral autonomy scrambled American parenting," *The Week*, theweek.com/parenting/1011854/ how-false-notions-of-moral-autonomy-scrambled-american-parenting
- Podcast Episode: Jason Thacker, "A conversation with Jay Y. Kim on discipleship in the digital age," jasonthacker.com/ podcast/a-conversation-with-jay-y-kim-on-discipleship-in-the-digital-age/

SESSION 4:

- Podcast Episode: Jason Thacker, "A conversation with Jonathan Rauch on misinformation and falsehood," jasonthacker.com/podcast/a-conversation-with-jonathan-rauch-on-misinformation-and-falsehood/
- Jason Thacker, "What is digital authoritarianism?" jasonthacker.com/2020/10/28/what-is-digital-authoritarianism/.
- Jason Thacker, "How social media has aided the disintegration of our public discourse," erlc.com/resource-library/articles/how-social-media-has-aided-the-disintegration-of-our-public-discourse/.
- Jason Thacker, "How deepfakes erode trust," erlc.com/resource-library/articles/how-deepfakes-erode-trust/.
- Jason Thacker, "3 words that will shape digital culture for good and cultivate virtue in the public square," erlc.com/resource-library/articles/3-words-that-will-shape-digital-culture-for-good-and-cultivate-virtue-in-the-public-square/.

SESSION 5

- Sherry Turkle, *Alone Together: Why We Expect More from Technology and Less from Each Other* (New York: Basic Books, 2017).
- Andy Crouch, *The Life We're Looking For: Reclaiming Relationship in a Technological World* (New York: Convergent Books, 2022).
- Jason Thacker, "What is our role in social media renewal?" erlc.com/resource-library/articles/what-is-our-role-in-social-media-renewal/.
- Benjamin E. Sasse, *Them: Why We Hate Each Other and How to Heal* (New York: St. Martin's Press, 2018).
- Jacob Shatzer, "Following @Jesus: Christian Discipleship in the Twenty-First Century" in Thacker, Jason, ed., *The Digital Public Square: Christian Ethics in a Technological Society.* (Nashville: B&H Academic, 2023).

SESSION 6

- Brett McCracken, *The Wisdom Pyramid: Feeding Your Soul in a Post-Truth World* (Wheaton: Crossway, 2021).
- Jason Thacker, *Following Jesus in a Digital Age* (Nashville: B&H Books, 2022).
- Jason Thacker, "Wisdom in the digital age," www.brnow.org/opinions/voices-opinion/wisdom-in-the-digital-age/.
- Jason Thacker, "Why should Christians study ethics?" erlc.com/resource-library/articles/why-should-christians-study-ethics/.

» END NOTES

1. Karen Hao, "Troll Farms Reached 140 Million Americans a Month on Facebook before 2020 Election, Internal Report Shows," MIT Technology Review, September 16, 2021, www.technologyreview.com/2021/09/16/1035851/. facebook-troll-farms-report-us-2020-election/.
2. For more on these five identities, see Jason Thacker, *Following Jesus in a Digital Age* (Nashville, TN: B&H Books, 2022), 124–132.
3. Timothy and Kathy Keller, *The Meaning of Marriage: Facing the Complexities of Commitment with the Wisdom of God* (New York: Dutton, 2011), 62.
4. Alan Jacobs, *Breaking Bread with the Dead: A Guide to a Tranquil Mind* (New York: Penguin Press, 2020), 12.
5. Sherry Turkle, *Alone Together: Why We Expect More from Technology and Less from Each Other* (New York: Basic Books, 2017), 17.
6. Neil Postman, *Amusing Ourselves to Death: Public Discourse in the Age of Show Business*, 20th Anniversary Edition (New York: Penguin Books, 2006), 99–100.

What does the Bible say about technology?

Available wherever books are sold

THE DIGITAL PUBLIC SQUARE:
CHRISTIAN ETHICS IN A TECHNOLOGICAL SOCIETY
Jason Thacker, editor

$27.99 // 9781087759821

AVAILABLE FEBRUARY 1, 2023

We now inhabit a digital world. Social media has changed and challenged some of our most basic understandings of truth, faith, and even the idea of a public square. In *The Digital Public Square*, editor Jason Thacker has chosen top Christian voices to help the church navigate the issues of censorship, conspiracy theories, sexual ethics, hate speech, religious freedom, and tribalism. In this unique work, David French, Patricia Shaw, and many others cast a distinctly Christian vision of a digital public theology to promote the common good throughout society.

Get the most from your study.

Are you ready to learn what the Bible says about technology and see how it may be shaping your walk with Christ?

In this study, you'll:

- · Get biblically informed wisdom for how to live in this digital age.
- · See how technology is subtly influencing your life, yourself, and your faith.
- · Discover how technology can aid or impede your discipleship and spiritual progress.
- · Establish habits and rhythms for healthy technology use.

STUDYING ON YOUR OWN?

Watch the teaching sessions, available via redemption code for individual video-streaming access, printed in this *Bible Study Book*.

LEADING A GROUP?

Each group member will need a *Following Jesus in a Digital Age Bible Study Book*, which includes video access. Because all participants will have access to the video content, you can choose to watch the videos outside of your group meeting if desired. Or, if you're watching together and someone misses a group meeting, they'll have the flexibility to catch up.

ADDITIONAL RESOURCES

BIBLE STUDY eBOOK WITH VIDEO ACCESS
The eBook includes the content of this printed book but offers the convenience and flexibility that comes with mobile technology.

005839204 **$19.99**

Browse study formats, a free session sample, video clips, church promotional materials, and more at lifeway.com/jesusindigitalage

Price and availability subject to change without notice.